WITHDRAWN

Walking Eye
mobile app

Discover the world's best destinations with the Insight Guides Walking Eye app, available to download for free in the App Store and Google Play.

The container app provides easy access to fantastic free content on events and activities taking place in your current location or chosen destination, with the possibility of booking, as well as the regularly-updated Insight Guides travel blog: Inspire Me. In addition, you can purchase curated, premium destination guides through the app, which feature local highlights, hotel, bar, restaurant and shopping listings, an A to Z of practical information and more. Or purchase and download Insight Guides eBooks straight to your device.

TOP 10 ATTRACTIONS

CASTELLO SFORZESCO
The impressive fortress is home to several museums. See page 44.

LA GALLERIA VITTORIO EMANUELE
Chic boutiques and cafés with elegant Belle Epoque facades. See page 37.

BASILICA DI SANT'AMBROGI
Milan's loveliest church. See page 68.

PINACOTECA DI BRERA
Home to one of the finest collections of Italian art, including The Kiss. See page 52.

QUADRILATERO D'ORO
All the big names in fashion have shops here. See page 56.

THE DUOMO
Walk among the spires and statues on the rooftop of the third-largest cathedral in Europe. See page 28.

THE BRERA
Bohemian yet quietly chic, this area of 'old Milan' conceals charming bars and cobblestoned corners. See page 51.

THE LAST SUPPER
Leonardo da Vinci's masterpiece is the jewel in the crown of Milan's many attractions. See page 62.

THE NAVIGLI
Restaurants and cafés line the banks in the quaint Canal Quarter, a nightlife centre. See page 69.

LA SCALA
Milan's world-famous opera house has been carefully restored to its full opulence. See page 38.

A PERFECT DAY

9.00am

Designer coffee
Café Trussardi, set in the Trussardi designer store overlooking La Scala, offers a coffee-and-brioche fix.

12 noon

Culture fix
Seek out the designer district's intriguing 'historic homes' museums, beginning with the Museo Poldi Pezzoli. This art-encrusted palace is a testament to the passion of a 19th-century aristocrat. The neighbouring Museo Bagatti Valsecchi is a tribute to the Renaissance.

10.00am

Chic shopping
Stroll along Via Manzoni to the Quadrilatero, the 'Golden Quadrangle' designer district. Call in (or window shop) at the Armani superstore (Via Manzoni 31) before exploring the boutiques on Via della Spiga and Via Montenapoleone. If flagging, stop for coffee and cakes at the old-fashioned Caffè Cova (Via Montenapoleone 8).

2.00pm

Lunch
Indulge in a leisurely lunch of creamy *risotto milanese* in Bice (Via Borgospesso 12; book) or choose lunch on the run from the contemporary Van Bol & Feste (Largo Cairoli).

6.30pm

Duomo sunset

Leave the park via the Cadorna exit and take the metro to the Duomo, Milan's great cathedral. Take the lift up to the top to admire the view, bathed in the light of the setting sun. Facing the Duomo is the Museo del Novecento (free entry every Tue from 2pm, Sun–Wed and Fri from 5.30pm, Thu and Sat from 8.30pm), a wonderful combination of 20th-century art and architectural games.

10.30pm

On the town

Tear yourself away from the sleek Principe Bar attached to Acanto, then head west to Corso Como, a vibrant nightlife area. Corso Como 10 is a perennially stylish spot for after-dinner drinks.

4.00pm

Park life

Largo Cairoli leads to the Castello Sforzesco, surrounded by Milan's most culture-studded park. See Michelangelo's unfinished masterpiece, the *Rondanini Pietà*, in the castle before strolling through Parco Sempione to the Triennale (Design Museum) for a sense of contemporary Milan.

8.00pm

Cocktail hour

Admire the cathedral spires over cocktails on the rooftop bars of La Rinascente store. Move on to the elegant Camparino, in the porticoes of the Galleria, a cocktail haunt since 1867.

9.00pm

Stylish dining

Acanto (Piazza della Repubblica; book) is one of Milan's most glamorous dining spots but, with its superb northern Italian cuisine, is far from being style over substance.

CONTENTS

INTRODUCTION

The old saying goes that for every church in Rome there's a bank in Milan. As the economic powerhouse of Italy, the northern city prides itself on efficiency and energy, and regards the Romans as idle and unproductive, distracted by the southern sun and gagged by the Vatican. Understandably perhaps, Milan sees itself as the true capital of Italy. Not only is it the industrial and financial capital, but it has forged ahead to become the country's most dynamic and influential city.

For decades now, Milan has been the leading fashion centre, the capital of publishing, media and design, and home to two top football teams. But to the Romans it remains a misty grey city, populated by slick yet unscrupulous workaholics.

THE RISE OF MILAN'S FASHION HOUSES

Milan has been making fabric since medieval times but its meteoric rise as the fashion capital only began in the 1950s, when it took over from Florence. The top designers found the dynamic metropolis more conducive to creativity, and Milan is now a base for Armani, Versace, Prada, Dolce & Gabbana and Gucci. Unsurprisingly, a futuristic 'Fashion City' is currently under construction in the emerging City Life district.

On Planet Fashion, you don't so much name-check the designer brands as breathe them, sip them, eat them, sleep them, and even live their dreams. All the designers are getting in on the lifestyle act, adding bars, spas or restaurants with gay abandon. You could wake up to a coffee in the Gucci Caffè in the Galleria or risk a close shave at the Dolce & Gabbana barber's. Armani, the master of minimalism, reigns supreme on Via Manzoni, with a superstore, club and chic eateries matched by a swish new hotel around the corner. Roberto Cavalli, where more is always more, responds with a fashion-victim café on Via della Spiga and his Just Cavalli supper club in Parco Sempione.

WORK HARD, PLAY HARD

Milan certainly has a strong work ethic, and is more in tune with a Northern European business centre than the typical Italian city of sunny piazzas and leisurely lunches. But it is by no means a city of all work and no play. *La dolce vita* is not played out in the same way as it is down south but for style and a contemporary buzz, no other Italian city comes close.

In the Quadrilatero d'Oro shopping quarter

As for cuisine, if you choose well, even fast food can be of Slow Food quality. Traditional inns offer hearty soups and stews, creamy risotto and stuffed pasta, as well as *charcuterie ossobucco* (veal shank) or gorgonzola and mascarpone cheeses. As for partying, the after-work *aperitivo* has become a Milanese way of life. Stylish bars serve sensational cocktails, with *stuzzichini* (snacks) and elegant canapés, while the old-fashioned *pasticcerie* (pastry shops) are equally enticing.

LA BELLA FIGURA

The city is synonymous with fashion, and the Milanese enjoy cutting-edge consumerism. Twice a year, at the opening of the world-famous fashion shows, the paparazzi descend on the city's hip hotels and cocktail bars. The stylish restaurants and sushi bars are then packed with celebrities, supermodels and fashionistas.

But at any time of year the locals cut a bella figura, and in the chic Quadrilatero d'Oro (Golden Quadrangle), where the

A leading city

'What happens in Milan will happen tomorrow in Italy. What is thought in Milan will be thought in Italy tomorrow.'
– Italian historian Gaetano Savemini.

designer boutiques provide a non-stop fashion show, the stores are more like art galleries than shops, and range from one-off boutiques to Slow Food superstores and designer megastores. At the glamorous Dolce & Gabbana on Corso Venezia, men's fashion comes with a barber and Martini bar. In the sleek Via Manzoni area now known as 'Armani-hood', the designer's neighbourhood is colonised by Armani branded clothes, chocolates, flowers, home furnishings, a café, club, sushi bar, and even an Armani hotel. Prices at these snooty spots are not for the faint-hearted, but there are plenty of more affordable shopping options along Corso Sempione, complemented by the arty boutiques in the Brera or quirky vintage in the Ticinese quarter.

CULTURAL CONFIDENCE

Milan may not offer the rich architectural heritage or homogeneity of Florence or Venice, but the city has a sumptuous Gothic cathedral, a historic castle in a leafy park, and one of the world's most prestigious opera houses. The Refectory of Santa Maria delle Grazie reveals what is arguably the most revered image in the Western world: Leonardo da Vinci's *The Last Supper*. Art museums range from the Pinacoteca di Brera and the Pinacoteca Ambrosiana, both filled with works by Italian masters, to intimate 'house museums' such as the Poldi-Pezzoli. Modern art is showcased in the exciting new Museum of the 19th Century while cutting-edge design can be found at the revamped Triennale.

Though little survives of medieval Milan, a pocket remains in Piazza Mercanti, whose Palazzo della Ragione attests to the wealth of the13th-century merchant city. During the Renaissance, Milan became a centre of art and culture, where geniuses such as Bramante created monuments while Leonardo (see page 21) adorned palaces and churches with great works of art. Navigable waterways were also created to link to the River Ticino in Switzerland and enable huge blocks of marble to be transported for the Duomo.

LOCATION AND QUALITY OF LIFE

Lying 50km (30 miles) south of the Alps in the heavily developed Po Valley, Milan is the capital of Lombardy, the most populous region in Italy. Milan's location makes it an ideal destination for excursions to neighbouring cities such as Pavia, Bergamo and Brescia. And should you need a break from bustling streets and cultural overload you can quickly escape – like the Milanese – to the tranquillity of the lakes and mountains, less than an hour away.

Tram passing La Scala opera house

The city itself covers an area of around 180 sq km (70 sq miles) and has a population of around 1.3 million, making it the second-largest city in Italy. With the suburbs included, the number swells to over 5.5 million. Milan is contained within a series of concentric circles radiating from the centre. The main historical monuments,

Patron saint

The Milanese refer to themselves as Ambrosiani, after Sant'Ambrogio (St Ambrose), patron saint of the city.

museums, galleries and exclusive shops are conveniently concentrated within the inner ring of boulevards, formerly a circle of canals (the Cerchia dei Navigli). The Spanish constructed a second perimeter in the mid-16th century by building city walls, extending 11km (7 miles) around the city and incorporating four main gateways. By the end of the 19th century, the city was bursting at the seams again, and the Spanish bastions and the gateways were gradually demolished to push the city further out. Today, the outermost ring road encompasses residential suburbs and industrial estates. The city is still expanding, and continues to attract waves of economic migrants, from other parts of Italy and further afield.

However, such popularity comes at a cost to quality of life. Milan has finally woken up to environmental concerns and has significantly improved its parks, particularly Parco Sempione, but has also created a new park in City Life. The canals, which already provide a brief respite from urban life, are being expanded to provide yet more access to landscaped parks via cycle lanes – as well as favouring leisurely boat trips on inland waterways developed by Leonardo da Vinci. In a bold move to combat pollution, the city has introduced a congestion charge system within the inner ring of boulevards. This, in turn, has encouraged cyclists to take to the roads. Such a positive response from most Milanese has led to the instigation of experimental 'no traffic days' when the city centre is awash with bicycles, and birdsong can once again be heard coming from palatial secret gardens. There is also a public car-sharing system, called GuidaMi, which discourages private ownership and promotes the use of electric vehicles. Contrary to its frenetic reputation, Milan is finally learning to relax.

A BRIEF HISTORY

Milan has a far longer history than its modern appearance might suggest. Strategically located on the trade route from the Alps to Rome, the city inevitably suffered the rampages of a succession of foreign rulers. The Celts were the first to invade, in the 6th century BC, followed by Romans, Huns, Goths, Lombards, Spaniards, Austrians and French. Despite invasions, sieges, plagues and, most recently, the bombardments of World War II, Milan has managed to emerge as Italy's wealthiest and most dynamic city.

ANCIENT MEDIOLANUM

According to Latin historian Livy, the foundation stone of Milan was laid in 603BC by a Celtic tribe from Gaul. The Romans called this wild barbaric region Gallia Cisalpina – Gaul this side of the Alps. In 222BC they put an end to Celtic forays, conquering Milan and other settlements in the Po Valley. Under Roman rule Milan became a thriving commercial centre, and in AD286, when Emperor Diocletian divided the Roman Empire, the town became the administrative seat of the West.

Emperor Constantine

In 313 Constantine the Great, ruler of the Western Roman Empire, signed the

Sant'Ambrogio, bishop of Milan

crucial Edict of Milan, granting Christians religious freedom. Under Sant'Ambrogio, the city's first bishop and patron saint, Milan became a leading religious centre.

HUNS, GOTHS AND LOMBARDS

The following centuries saw a decline in the city's fortunes as it was ravaged by waves of invaders. First came Attila the Hun, destroying Milan in 452. Following the breakdown of the Roman Empire in the West a quarter of a century later, Milan, along with the rest of Italy, was subject to invasions by the Goths. Odoacer, a general in the army of the Western Roman Empire, crowned himself king in 476 in Italy's new capital at Pavia but was murdered at a banquet by his rival, Theodoric the Ostrogoth. In 568 another warfaring Germanic tribe, the Longobardi (Lombards) seized the main cities north of the Po. Their leader, King Alboin, established his court at Pavia but was murdered by his wife, Rosamunda (whom he had forced to drink wine from her dead father's skull). However, the Lombards gradually renounced their barbarian ways and were assimilated, adopting Roman customs, intermarrying and even converting to Christianity.

Lombardy became part of the Carolingian Empire under Charlemagne and flourished, particularly in the late 9th and 10th centuries when splendid churches were constructed.

THE COMMUNE OF MILAN

Milan became a commune – an independent city-state. Struggle for supremacy ensued but Milan prevailed in wars against its rivals, Pavia, Cremona, Como and Lodi. However, the destruction of Como gave the Holy Roman Emperor, Frederick Barbarossa, the pretext to reclaim the city in 1162, after a nine-month siege. Five years later Milan joined other communes in the new Lombard League, the northern Italian separatist movement, which defeated Barbarossa at Legnano, northwest of Milan, in 1176. Barbarossa was forced to sign the Peace of Constance in 1183, which recognised the authority of the city-states of northern Italy, including Milan.

LORDS OF MILAN: THE VISCONTI AND SFORZA

Internal power struggles led to the decline of the communes, and the 13th century saw the rise of the great dynasties, notably the noble Visconti, who held sway over Milan until 1477. In the factionalism that characterised the period, the Visconti supported the Ghibellines (who favoured the German emperor) while their arch-rivals, the Torriani, supported the Guelphs (who favoured the Pope).

From 1395, the Visconti were dukes of the city, and it was under Gian Galeazzo Visconti (1351–1402) that the duchy

SANT'AMBROGIO

St Ambrose (Sant'Ambrogio) is a cult figure to the Milanese. Legend has it that shortly after Ambrogio's birth in 340 a swarm of bees descended on his face, leaving a drop of honey on his lips and prophesying his future gift as a honey-tongued orator – hence the bees and beehives in the saint's iconography.

reached its zenith. Through military conquest and diplomacy, he expanded Milan's territories to cover most of northern Italy, extending as far as Pisa, Siena, Perugia and Bologna. However, as the duke was mustering his forces against Florence, he succumbed to the plague and died. A man of great cultural and religious ambition, Gian Galeazzo oversaw the foundation of Milan's cathedral and castle, and the great Certosa (Carthusian monastery) at Pavia.

In 1447, following a threat from a Venetian army, his son, Filippo Maria, sought military assistance from his son-in-law, the *condottiere* (mercenary) Francesco Sforza. This heralded a century of rule by the next great dynasty, the Sforza. Francesco's eldest son, Galeazzo Maria Sforza, though extravagant and dissolute, was an able leader who introduced the cultivation of rice and mulberries. Under his rule, industry also flourished, particularly the manufacture of textiles and arms. Furthermore, he was a patron of leading artists and scholars, who glorified the Sforza name. The duke was murdered in 1476 on the steps of Milan's San Gottardo in Corte chapel by aggrieved court officials.

One of Castello Sforzesco's towers

LUDOVICO IL MORO

The most celebrated Sforza ruler was Ludovico, who

usurped power through the regency of his seven-year-old nephew, Gian Galeazzo Maria. Known as Ludovico il Moro (the Moor) on account of his swarthy complexion and black hair, he was one of the great princes of the Renaissance. In his day, there were five superpowers in Italian politics: the Papacy, the kingdom of Naples and Sicily, Florence, Venice and Milan. It was the era of equilibrium politics, when each superstate strove for survival or supremacy by duplicitous diplomacy.

The Visconti coat of arms

Ludovico, a past master of the art, hated the burgeoning power of his nearest rival, Venice, but courted the support of Florence. He struck alliances with the two great powers of Continental Europe, France and the Holy Roman Empire, to prevent reinstatement of the true heir to the dukedom. Later he made an alliance with Venice against France with the marriage of his niece, Bianca Maria, to the Holy Roman Emperor, Maximilian, and chose for himself the beautiful 15-year-old Beatrice d'Este, daughter of the Duke of Ferrara. From Maximilian he purchased the dukedom of Milan and, with his wife, maintained one of the most elegant courts in Europe.

Under Ludovico's patronage leading artists and architects were commissioned to create monuments and adorn palaces and churches. Leonardo da Vinci, the Tuscan-born Renaissance man, ran a flourishing workshop, worked as

Statue of Leonardo da Vinci on Piazza della Scala

military architect to the duke, designed court festivals and produced groundbreaking artistic, scientific and medical studies. *The Last Supper* is one of the few of his paintings that survive in the city.

Initiating the chaotic period of European intervention in Italian politics, Charles VIII of France attempted to conquer Naples in 1494, prompting Ludovico to join a Venetian alliance to expel the French from Italy. On Charles's death, Louis XII claimed the duchy of Milan as a descendant of the first Visconti duke. Ludovico was expelled, with the encouragement of the populace who by now had tired of his policy of high taxation. In 1500 he attempted to reclaim the city, but his conscript Swiss and German armies refused to support him when the critical moment came, and he was exiled to France, where he spent the rest of his life.

FOREIGN INTERVENTION

The great struggle between France and Habsburg Spain for dominance in Italy effectively ended at the battle of Pavia in 1525, when the French were expelled from the duchy of Milan. The state of Milan was briefly restored to the Sforza dynasty, but, on the death of Francesco II in 1535, the duchy fell under the domination of the Spanish Habsburg emperor Charles V, who later granted it to his son, the future Philip II of Spain. From the golden age of the duchy, Milan underwent the dark age of Spanish domination. It was to last 170 years – an era of complete stagnation, reaching its lowest ebb with the devastating plague of 1630.

Economic revival had to wait until the Spanish rulers were driven out by the Austrians in the War of the Spanish Succession. Austrian occupation was to last, almost uninterrupted, from 1706 until 1859. Although notoriously

LEONARDO IN MILAN

Leonardo da Vinci is inextricably linked to Milan, even if Milan is rarely linked to the Renaissance. Apart from his celebrated *Last Supper* and the ingenious inventions on display in the Museum of Science, Leonardo, with his enthusiasm for hydraulic engineering, also designed the complex locks in Milan's Navigli canals, using devices still used today. Leonardo was the complete Renaissance man, at home with art, astronomy, mechanics and warfare.

In case his reputation hadn't preceded him, Leonardo sent Ludovico Sforza, ruler of Milan, his compelling CV: 'I can construct bridges (and) a kind of cannon with which to hurl small stones like hail. I can noiselessly construct subterranean passages. I can make armoured wagons (and) can give you as complete satisfaction as anyone else in the construction of buildings.' Finally, almost as an afterthought, Leonardo adds: 'Also, in painting, I can do as much as anyone, whoever he may be.'

Biblioteca Ambrosiana (www.ambrosiana.eu), the late 16th-century library and picture gallery, houses the polymath's *Codex Atlanticus* folios and a superb art collection, including his only known portrait painting of a man: *The Musician*.

despotic, the rulers collaborated with the emerging merchant classes, fostering 50 years of growth. The reign of the enlightened Empress Maria Theresa saw major economic and social reforms and the rise of splendid neoclassical monuments, such as the Teatro alla Scala and the Palazzo Reale (Royal Palace).

The French returned in 1796, with Napoleon Bonaparte's armies sweeping into Milan. Napoleon had the full support of the Milanese bourgeoisie, and the Austrians were chased out. Milan became capital of the Cisalpine Republic, and Napoleon was crowned king of Italy in the Duomo in 1805. But Milan – along with the rest of Lombardy and most of Italy – was soon to fall again to the Austrians. This time it was a hated regime, and in 1848, when revolution swept through Italy, Milan was the scene of the Cinque Giornate (Five Days) revolt. Control was regained, but by then the tide of the Risorgimento (Italian Unification Movement) was virtually unstoppable. In 1859 the troops of Vittorio Emanuele and Napoleon III of France defeated the Austrians at Magenta and Solferino, and entered Milan in triumph.

FROM UNIFICATION TO TODAY

By 1870 Italy was finally united. Vittorio Emanuele became the first king of Italy, and Rome was declared capital of the new kingdom. Rapid growth and industrialisation characterised the post-unification period. Milan became the economic and cultural capital of Italy, and over a period of 50 years the population trebled. But with growth came social tension, and the first socialist party was founded in Milan in 1882. Following World War I, political and economic upheavals led to the birth of Fascism, symbolised by Milan's monolithic Central Station. It was in Milan that Mussolini created Europe's first Fascist party in 1919. Milan was part of Mussolini's unsuccessful puppet government at Salò on Lake Garda from 1943–5. Following his capture and execution in 1945, Mussolini was brought to Milan and put on display, alongside his mistress, Clara Petacci, at a petrol station in Piazzale Loreto.

As a key industrial centre, Milan suffered devastating bombardments from Allied air raids during World War II. However, a major reconstruction programme followed, and in the 1950s the city became an industrial powerhouse, forming with Genoa and Turin the 'Industrial Triangle' of Italy. Migrants flocked in from southern Italy, taking up jobs in the factories of Fiat, Alfa Romeo and Pirelli. By the 1980s, a thriving service economy meant that Milan was not only Italy's commercial and financial hub, but the country's capital for publishing, media, fashion and design.

In the early 1990s the city was the focus of the great political scandal dubbed *Tangentopoli* (Bribesville). Extensive

Piazza della Scala as it was in 1880

investigations, known as the *Mani Pulite* (Clean Hands), exposed political corruption on a massive scale, and led to the accusation of eight former prime ministers and around 5,000 businessmen. Further scandal engulfed the city again under the decadent last premiership of media magnate Silvio Berlusconi, who resigned in 2011 to make way for a technocratic government of national unity.

Despite the sleaze and corruptions of the Berlusconi era, Milan has survived the scandals and forged ahead as an economic powerhouse in its own right. After winning its bid to host Expo 2015 – just over a century since it hosted its last world fair – Milan launched an ambitious urban development programme. Fieramilano, already the largest trade exhibition centre in Europe, was expanded further. Much of Fieramilanocity, the old city centre fairground site was redeveloped to make space for the CityLife project, and now features skyscrapers, a park and new museums, including the Museum of Contemporary Art, designed by Daniel Libeskind. CityLife, including its three designer towers and the metro station of the same name, was designed by Zaha Hadid, Isozaki and Libeskind. The Navigli canal network is also being expanded, along with Milan's metro network. The Expo itself, which focused on sustainability, food and energy, attracted over 22 million visitors to this cutting-edge city. The hope is that, despite the current banking crisis and a growing pollution problem, the Expo has signalled a new era for Milan and its region.

Italian flag flies in the Navigli (canal) district

HISTORICAL LANDMARKS

603BC Milan founded by the Gauls.

222BC Romans occupy Milan.

AD286 Milan becomes capital of the Western Roman Empire.

452 Attila the Hun plunders Milan.

563 Milan is razed by the Goths.

568 Invasion of the Lombards.

774 Charlemagne brings Lombard rule to an end.

1045 Milan becomes a free commune, or city-state.

1162 Frederick Barbarossa brings the city under Imperial control.

1176 Lombard League defeats Barbarossa at Legnano.

1183 Milan regains independence.

1447 Milan becomes one of the leading cities of the Renaissance.

1535 Milan falls to Spain.

1629–31 The plague devastates Milan.

1706 Milan is ceded to Austria.

1796 Napoleon makes Milan capital of his Cisalpine Republic.

1815 Congress of Vienna gives Milan again to the Austrians.

1848 Cinque Giornate revolt in Milan; Austrians re-enter Milan.

1859 Austrians defeated at the Battle of Magenta; troops of Vittorio Emanuele and France re-enter Milan.

1919 Mussolini founds the first Fascist party in Milan.

1943 Milan suffers heavy bombardment in World War II.

1945 Mussolini is executed and his body strung up in Milan.

2001 Coalition headed by Silvio Berlusconi wins general election.

2004 The Teatro alla Scala reopens after a three-year renovation.

2011 Milan's Museo del Novecento (Museum of the 20th century) opens to great acclaim.

2012 Milan introduces a congestion charge to decrease pollution and the Central Station is revamped.

2015 Milan hosts the Expo Universal Exhibition. Construction of *Il Dritto* (Allianz Tower), part of the CityLife project, is completed.

2016 Giuseppe Sala is elected Milan's new mayor. Chinese company Suning Commerce Group takes over Inter Milan football club.

WHERE TO GO

Milan's cathedral, known as the Duomo, is the city symbol. Begun in 1386, it has been in continual evolution ever since. Indeed, 'As long as the building of the Duomo' is a typical Milanese expression. Much like the Duomo, Milan is a work in progress, building with more panache than anywhere else in Italy, for good or ill.

Milan is currently doubling the reach of its metro system, creating new expressways and upgrading its railways. New galleries continue to open, such as the impressive Museum of Cultures (MUDEC) and the Armani/Silos, both of which were inaugurated in 2015. Dilapidated industrial areas are being transformed, and Futuristic districts created, such as 'Fashion City', near Garibaldi station, and the 'City Life' centre on the site of the old trade fair. The Expo 2015 relaunched Milan as a model of urban renewal, but elsewhere historical districts, such as the bohemian Navigli canal quarter, have also been given a facelift, along with the adjoining Zona Tortona design district.

Yet 'old Milan' survives, whether in the elegant area around the Cathedral, and its enveloping galleries, or in the romantic Brera district, where bohemian bars overlook charming churches. As for the arty Navigli, when sitting in a rustic waterside inn, with the faint rumble of trams beyond, it feels like you've been transported from the consumerist Milanese metropolis to timeless provincial Italy. Even the fashion district is home to several intimate art museums that would do Tuscany credit. Throughout the city, cutting-edge restaurants are outnumbered by cosy inns, *grande-dame* hotels and old-fashioned patisserie shops. The Milanese love tradition as much as they love change.

The lofty Galleria Vittorio Emanuele II

GETTING AROUND

The historic heart of the city is surprisingly compact, with the main arteries fanning out from the great Gothic Duomo and La Scala opera house: northwest to the imposing Castello Sforzesco and Parco Sempione, northeast to the Quadrilatero d'Oro fashion district, north to the arty neighbourhood of the Brera. To the west lies the smart Corso Magenta, with Santa Maria delle Grazie's *The Last Supper* by Leonardo, and to the south, the hip Navigli canal quarter. The main attractions of the city can be covered in a few days, usually on foot, but with some short journeys by tram or metro necessary.

THE DUOMO AND HISTORIC CENTRE

The Duomo (metro Duomo) is the geographical and spiritual heart of the city, so is a natural magnet and the best place to explore first. The historic centre, the *centro storico,* also provides a representative mix of art museums and Milanese architecture, ranging from the majestic cathedral to La Scala opera house and the Galleria Vittorio Emanuele, one of Europe's most elegant shopping galleries. That's in addition to the Pinacoteca Ambrosiana's atmospheric art collection and your first contact with Leonardo da Vinci.

Following most of these suggestions makes for cultural overload so try to do as the Milanese do, and be tempted along the way by the distinctive bars and cafés that bring this area to life. Some are mentioned below, but depending on the time of day, there are fuller listings in Restaurants (see page 108), Lunch Milanese-style (see page 98) and Night-life (see page 92).

DUOMO

Dominating the heart of the city, and soaring over the central square, is the Gothic **Duomo** ❶ (cathedral, www.duomo

milano.it; daily 8am–7pm; roof, daily 9am–7pm; Duomo Pass provides entry to the cathedral, terrace, museum and the San Gottardo church). The Duomo Info Point is right behind the cathedral at the porch of the Church of Santa Maria Annunciata in Camposanto (tel: 02 7202 3375; Mon–Sat 9.30am–5.30pm, Sun 11am–3pm).

Nothing quite prepares you for the first sight of the monumental facade. This is the third-largest church in Europe, after the cathedral in Seville and St Peter's in Rome. The area covers 12,000 sq m (130,000 sq ft), the capacity is around 40,000, and the facade is adorned with a forest of 3,000 statues, 135 spires and 96 gargoyles.

Begun in 1386, the Duomo was the brainchild of Duke Gian Galeazzo Visconti, whose aim was to create the greatest church in Christendom. The then bishop of Milan, Antonio da Saluzzo, declared a Jubilee to persuade the Milanese to help

Exploring the roof terraces of the Duomo

fund or assist the colossal project. Armourers, drapers, boot-makers and other artisans all lent a hand, while French and German architects, engineers and sculptors, well versed in the Gothic tradition, worked alongside local craftsmen. At one stage, there were around 300 sculptors from all over Europe chiselling away in the cathedral workshops.

The original plan was a building in Lombard terracotta, but Gian Galeazzo changed his mind and decided the entire structure was to be clad in pale but peachy Candoglia marble. This entailed the construction of roads and canals to drag the great blocks of marble from the quarries near Lake Maggiore.

The Madonnina

A much-loved symbol of the city, the Madonnina (below), atop the Duomo, is 4.46m (14.5ft) high. She was placed on the church's tallest spire in 1774, and remained the highest point in the city until the Pirelli skyscraper was built in the late 1950s (see page 13). The clergy were none too pleased that she had lost her superior position, so a replica was placed on top of the Pirelli Tower.

Despite the huge workforce it was to be more than five centuries before the cathedral was completed. The result is a hybrid of Renaissance, Gothic and Baroque styles, with 19th-century additions. The work on the facade, which dates from the 17th century, gave rise to decades of controversy, and was only finished in 1812 under Napoleon.

Even on a dull day the marble facade looks strikingly bright, almost blindingly so since its recent facelift has left it a lovely

The Duomo has a pillar for every week of the year

peachy-pink colour that changes according to the light. Before entering the church, admire the Gothic apse. Built in 1386–1447, and decorated with sculptures and tracery, this is the oldest part of the Duomo.

While here, traipse up to the **Terrazzi** (roof terraces) by clambering up the 158 steps, or else take the lift. Apart from sensational views of the city and, on those rare, very clear days, as far as the Matterhorn, you can walk among the forest of spires, statues, turrets and gargoyles and get a closer look at the gilded figure of the **Madonnina** (Little Madonna), which crowns the cathedral.

INSIDE THE CATHEDRAL

From the dazzling white piazza you are plunged into the dimly lit, spartan interior, enlivened by a new, glittering glass book-shop. The five aisles are divided by 52 **colossal piers** – one for every week of the year – their capitals decorated with 15th-century figures of saints and prophets.

Works of art within the church include sarcophagi, funerary shrines and statues, the most famous of which is the gruesome, anatomical *Statue of St Bartholomew Flayed* (1562) in the right transept, depicting the saint carrying his own skin. At the end of the transept lies the elaborate marble tomb of Gian Giacomo Medici, by Leone Leoni (1509–90), a pupil of Michelangelo. This was commissioned in 1564 by Pope Pius IV, the brother of Gian Giacomo. Unconnected with the Florentine Medici and nicknamed *Il Medeghino* (Little Medico), Gian Giacomo was from a Milanese family but was banished from the city after committing a murder. He fled to Lake Como and acquired his wealth from privateering and working as a *condottiere* (mercenary) in the service of Charles V. A large sum donated to the Duomo, plus family connections, ensured this prominent funerary monument. In the left transept the seven-branched bronze **Trivulzio Candelabrum,** the work of a medieval goldsmith, is adorned with monsters and mythical figures representing the arts, crafts and virtues.

The church is illuminated by beautiful **stained-glass windows**, dating from the 15th–20th centuries, which are fully lit up from within at the weekend. The oldest is the fifth window in the right-hand aisle, illustrating scenes from the *Life of Christ*. The beautiful Gothic windows of the apse are decorated with 19th-century scenes from both the Old and New Testaments. The permanently shining red light in the vault of the Duomo marks the place of a nail said to be from

Stained-glass window in the cathedral

Piazza del Duomo

Christ's cross. On the second Sunday in September, the bishop of Milan is hoisted up to the vault to bring the nail down from its niche for public view.

A stairway behind the main altar leads down to the **Treasury**, housing a priceless collection of gold, silverwork and holy vestments. In the neighbouring **Crypt** (1606), a rock crystal urn contains the body of San Carlo Borromeo (1538–84), clad in full regalia. Archbishop and cardinal of Milan, he was a leading light of the Catholic Counter-Reformation and was canonised in 1610. A staircase near the Duomo entrance leads down to the remains of the 4th-century **Baptistery** on what was then pavement level. It was here that Sant'Ambrogio is said to have baptised St Augustine.

PIAZZA DEL DUOMO

The gigantic central piazza, milling with people and pigeons, is awe-inspiring, but lacks the carefree charm of a typical Italian *piazza*. No cafés spill onto the square, but the historic

The remaining campanile of the Church of San Gottardo in Corte

Camparino is tucked under the porticoes, created by the founder of the Campari dynasty in 1867. It was here, at the entrance to Galleria Vittorio Emanuele, that Verdi used to enjoy a drink after concerts and where, in 1877, Milanese nobility flocked to see the first experiment in electric lighting on the piazza. It was also here, in this Art Nouveau interior, that stressed Milanese still relax over a coffee or Campari, served with over-sized olives. Camparino makes a good start to any evening promenade (see page 93).

The only landmark on the piazza, apart from the big red Ms of the metro, is Ercole Rosa's 1896 equestrian statue of Vittorio Emanuele II, first king of Italy, who triumphantly entered Milan in 1859. Despite the piazza seeming uninviting, its monuments are impressive, particularly the new Museo del Novecento.

The Palazzo Reale (Royal Palace; www.palazzorealemilano. it; Mon 2.30–7.30pm, Tue–Wed, Fri and Sun 9.30am–7.30pm, Thu–Sat until 10.30pm) on the south side of the Duomo stands on the site of the original Broletto or town hall, destroyed by Frederick Barbarossa in 1162. It was rebuilt in 1171, then later transformed into the Ducal Palace for the Visconti and Sforza dynasties. On the occasion of Galeazzo Visconti's marriage to Beatrice d'Este in Modena, their entry into Milan was marked by eight days of festivities at the palace. In 1336 the Church of San Gottardo in Corte was built as the Visconti's private chapel. You can still see the charming colonnaded campanile rising to the rear of the palace, but the church itself was destroyed when the building was incorporated into the neoclassical palace. In 1412 the church steps were the scene of the murder of Giovanni Maria Visconti. As a consequence the family decided to reside in the safer environs of the fortified castle. Under the Sforza a theatre was established at the palace, and in 1595 Mozart, who was only 14, performed here.

The current neoclassical aspect of the Palazzo Reale dates from the transformation during the late 18th century, when Empress Maria Theresa of Austria chose Giuseppe Piermarini to remodel the building in neoclassical style, with sumptuously decorated rooms. The palace suffered devastation during the Allied bombardments of 1943, and only recently has been re-opened to its citizens, fully restored, bar an unfinished costume museum. While not one of Milan's greatest sights, the palace is definitely worth seeing if you are visiting an art exhibition or keen to see the changing styles under the Austrians, the French and the Italian house of Savoy.

The palace showcases blockbuster art exhibitions (visit www.turismo.milano.it for event information). The rooms are restored in styles that characterise court life in 1781–1860 and can be seen in the **Museo della Reggia**. The east wing of the Palazzo Reale houses the **Grande**

The serpent is the symbol of Milan

Museo del Duomo (Cathedral Museum; http://museo.duomo milano.it; Thu–Tue 10am–6pm). The collection charts the history of the Duomo, including a section on how the Madonnina got to the top of the highest spire in 1774, accompanied by displays of the cathedral's original statuary and stained glass, transferred here for safekeeping.

Part of the Palazzo Reale was demolished in the late 1930s to make way for the three-storey Arengario building, which is now the captivating **Museo del Novecento** ❷ (Museum of the 20th Century; www.museodelnovecento.org; Mon 2.30–7.30pm, Tue–Wed, Fri and Sun 9.30am–7.30pm, Thu and Sat until 10.30pm). The collection ranges from the avant-garde Futurist movement to works from the early 1980s. In pride of place are works by Futurists of the stature of Boccioni and Carra, and Metaphysical artists such as Giorgio di Chirico

MILAN'S SERPENTINE SYMBOL

A serpent devouring a child is one of the Visconti family symbols (you can spot it on the frescoed ceilings of the Castello Sforzesco, see page 45). The derivation of the symbol remains a mystery. It could represent the dragon which, according to legend, terrorised Milan in the early 5th century and was slaughtered by Uberto of Angera, founder of the Visconti, or it could reflect the snake talisman that the Lombards used to wear around their necks.

You can see the symbol all over the city – particularly on the Alfa Romeo logo. When Romano Cattaneo, an Alfa draughtsman, was waiting for a tram in Piazza Castello in 1910, he drew inspiration for the logo of the new Milan-based company from the serpent coat of arms embellishing the castle gateway. On the left side of the Alfa Romeo logo is a red cross on a white background, symbol of Milan.

and Filippo De Pisis. The building, designed in 'Fascist lite' style, has been beautifully adapted to its new purpose, and the chic café has already become a popular meeting place.

GALLERIA VITTORIO EMANUELE II

Linking Piazza del Duomo and Piazza della Scala is the pedestrianised **Galleria Vittorio Emanuele II** ❸ (or 'La Galleria'), a light, airy, glass-and-iron shopping arcade that is one of the most elegant ever created. The cruciform Galleria, built in honour of Austrian Emperor Franz Joseph, was the work of architect Giuseppe Mengoni, who plunged to his death from the scaffolding on the site months before it was completed in 1878. More cheerfully, this gracious rendez-vous, known as *il salotto di Milano* (Milan's drawing room), is flanked by a discreet luxury hotel, and by chic cafés, restaurants and designer boutiques, many of which have Belle Epoque facades. Savini is the oldest restaurant, and has been welcoming stars from La Scala since 1867. Prada has been here since 1913, while Louis Vuitton and Gucci are more recent arrivals, with the Gucci café a popular people-watching spot. For somewhere more relaxed, but with lofty views, retreat to the rooftops of La Rinascente around the corner (see page 109).

Palazzo Reale

Pavement mosaic in La Galleria

TEATRO ALLA SCALA

The sombre neoclassical facade of the world-famous opera house gives no hint of the fabulously opulent auditorium. More popularly known as **La Scala** ❹, this is arguably the world's most celebrated opera house. Few opera houses command such an exacting set of fans, who don't hesitate to show their disapproval if a singer fails to impress.

Many top names in Italian opera have made their debuts here, among them Puccini, Verdi and Bellini. Commissioned in 1776–8 by Empress Maria Theresa of Austria, it was designed by Giuseppe Piermarini and built on the site of a former theatre which was destroyed by fire in 1776. The new theatre was named after the church of Santa Maria alla Scala, which originally stood here. La Scala suffered serious damage during the 1943 air raids, but, symbolically, it became the first city structure to be rebuilt. The reopening was celebrated with a memorable concert conducted by the renowned conductor Toscanini, who returned from America after a 17-year absence.

Provided there are no rehearsals going on, you can peep into the auditorium on a visit to the **Museo Teatrale alla Scala** (Scala Theatre Museum; www.teatroallascala.org; daily 9am–12.30pm, 1.30–5.30pm). The neoclassical rooms display portraits and busts of famous opera singers and composers, stage designs, musical instruments and operatic memorabilia.

In the centre of **Piazza della Scala** the bearded figure on the pedestal is Leonardo da Vinci, surrounded by four of his pupils. Facing the Teatro alla Scala, the splendid **Palazzo Marino** was built for a wealthy Genoese financier, Tommaso Marino, in 1558 and given a new facade in the late 19th century. Today, this is the Town Hall, and you can arrange a guided tour (Mon and Thu, prior booking only). Alternatively, peek through the grill into the Courtyard of Honour from Via Marina, which leads into Piazza San Fedele. Also overlooking the square is the **Galleria d'Italia** (see page 59), but leave it for another day to avoid art overload.

In front of the Baroque church of San Fedele stands a statue of Alessandro Manzoni (1785–1873), author of the plodding but renowned *I Promessi Sposi (The Betrothed)*. This worthy set-text for Italian students is set in Lombardy during the oppressive Spanish rule in the 17th century, and evokes the plague of 1630, which devastated Milan. Born in the city in 1814, Manzoni lived in the nearby Piazza Belgioioso, at the **Casa di Alessandro Manzoni** (www.casadelmanzoni.it; Tue–Fri 10am–6pm, Sat 2pm–6pm; free) until his death after a fall on the steps of the San Fedele church. The entrance is behind San Fedele in Via Omenoni, named after the eight *telamones* (figures as pillars) that characterise the **Casa degli Omenoni**.

Take a spin

The colourful pavement mosaics under the glass dome of the Galleria depict the coat of arms of the Savoys and the symbols of four cities: Milan (red cross on a white background), Turin (bull), Florence (lily) and Rome (she-wolf). Tradition has it that spinning your heels on the bull's well-worn testicles will bring good luck.

PIAZZA MERCANTI

In contrast to the Piazza del Duomo, the neighbouring **Piazza Mercanti** ❺ is an intimate square that was left relatively unscathed by urban development and wartime bombardment. The former political and administrative centre of the city, it is only half its original size, but it preserves the medieval **Palazzo della Ragione** (1233), a fine porticoed brick building which was formerly the Broletto (law courts). It was built by Oldrado da Tresseno, the *podestà* (mayor) depicted in an equestrian relief on the piazza side of the palace. Between the second and third arches stands a relief of the half-woolly wild boar *(scrofa semilanuta)*, symbol of the city in ancient times.

On the other side of the square is the lovely **Loggia degli Osii**, the grey-and-white-striped marble building where banns were declared. The coats of arms displayed on the facade represent the powerful local families of the day. The loggia of the **Palazzo della Ragione Fotografia** (www.palazzodellaragionefotografia.it) used to shelter medieval market stalls; today temporary photographic exhibitions are held here. On the piazza an old well survives, and tables spill on to the square from the charming Al Mercante, a tempting lunch spot from which to admire the remnants of medieval Milan (see page 108).

Casa di Alessandro Manzoni

AMBROSIANA GALLERY AND LIBRARY

The **Pinacoteca Ambrosiana** ❻ (Ambrosian Gallery; Piazza Pio XI; tel: 02 8069 2215;

La Scala's two-ton, 900-light chandelier lowered for its annual clean

www.ambrosiana.eu; Tue–Sun 10am–6pm) is an unmissable museum of the Old Masters featuring a Leonardo-filled library. As such, it is both an art collection second only to the Pinacoteca di Brera, and an opportunity to see Leonardo da Vinci drawings in a hushed, atmospheric, deeply Milanese setting. The building is a fine example of late 16th-century Lombard architecture, with mullioned windows, frescoed walls and vaulted ceilings.

In 1609 Cardinal Federico Borromeo commissioned the **Biblioteca Ambrosiana** (Ambrosian Library) to house his huge array of manuscripts, prints and books, and private art collection. As a patron of the arts, he donated this outstanding collection to the Ambrosian Foundation in 1618, a collection that has been further enriched over the centuries. The Biblioteca is reputedly the first public library in Italy. Some might say that it's been downhill ever since as Italians are no longer dedicated readers, and much prefer the visual arts, which carry more prestige. But

Piazza Mercanti

the Leonardo folios combine both drawings and written observations.

The highlights of the Ambrosian gallery are the first rooms, containing numerous works from Federico's original private collection. Masterpieces include: Titian's *Adoration of the Magi* (Room 1); *The Musician* (Room 2), depicting a musician in the Sforza Court and attributed to Leonardo da Vinci; Raphael's cartoon for the *School of Athens* fresco in the Vatican (Room 5); and Caravaggio's famous *Basket of Fruit* (Room 6), of which Federico wrote, 'I would have liked to have put another similar basket next to it, but as nobody could equal the beauty and incomparable excellence of this one, it remained alone.' There are also paintings by Botticelli, Ghirlandaio, Bergognone, Luino and Bramantino, along with Flemish and Dutch art. The visit ends in the library, with the largest extant collection of Leonardo's drawings and designs. Known as the *Codex Atlanticus*, the collection has been in the Ambrosiana since 1637, but can only now be seen properly, with the folios displayed on a rotational basis. The *Codex* is a window into the mind of a true Renaissance man. On display might be drawings of war devices, flying machines, canal sluice gates, sketches of bombardments, or anatomical and botanical studies.

SANTA MARIA PRESSO SAN SATIRO

You could easily miss Santa Maria Presso San Satiro, a gem tucked away south of the Piazza del Duomo (Via Speronari 3; Mon–Fri 7.30–11.30am, 3.30–6.30pm, Sat 3.30–7pm, Sun 10am–noon and 3.30–7pm). Legend has it that a fresco of the *Madonna and Child*, which decorated the 9th-century chapel of San Satiro, shed blood when it was vandalised in 1242. Bramante later remodelled the chapel and provided a safe haven for the fresco, which you can see on the high altar. The architect ingeniously created the impression of depth by devising a *trompe l'oeil* apse.

The Cappella della Pietà (off the left transept) has early medieval frescoes and a terracotta *Pietà* (1482) by Agosto De Fondutis; there are more of his terracottas in the lovely baptistery. Bramante's plans for the facade never materialised, the present one being 19th-century neo-Renaissance. The beautiful bell tower at the back of the church, seen from Via Falcone, is one of the oldest in Lombardy.

If feeling peckish, consider a light lunch at Ottimo Massimo, Peck, or Eat's Store, or a leisurely affair in Al Mercante or Boeucc, for an

Biblioteca Ambrosiana

old-school Milanese atmosphere (see Historic Centre restaurants, see page 108).

CASTELLO SFORZESCO AND THE NORTHWEST

The monumental **Castello Sforzesco** (metro Cairoli) was the stronghold and residence of the mighty Milanese dynasties, the Visconti and Sforza. Dating from 1360 and extended over the centuries, it is the city's largest historical complex, and stands as a symbol of the dramatic events of Milan's history. The rambling Parco Sempione, stretching from the castle to the Arco della Pace, was formerly a Sforza hunting reserve but has been a park since the late 19th century.

IL GRAN CAVALLO

In 1482 Ludovico Sforza, duke of Milan, commissioned Leonardo da Vinci to create a 7m (24ft) -high bronze horse, which was to be the largest equestrian statue ever conceived and Leonardo's most important work. The multi-talented artist, who was busy producing city plans for Milan, a defence system for the castle, additions to the canal network and costumes for ducal entertainments, took years to complete the full-scale clay model. By the time it was finished, war with the French was imminent, and the bronze designated for the monument was cast into cannons. French troops arrived in 1499, and the colossal model was used for target practice by their archers.

In 1999, a bronze replica of the equestrian monument was erected in San Siro. This suburb of Milan, once fields and orchards, was the designated area for the original bronze. Conceived and cast in the US, the horse was sculpted according to Leonardo's notes and drawings, and was donated to Milan in appreciation 'of the genius of Leonardo and the legacy of the Italian Renaissance'.

Milan's skyline, with Castello Sforzesco in the foreground, and the Duomo's spires in the distance

Parco Sempione was landscaped in 1893 in so-called English style, which, in Italy, is often a euphemism for a romantic but slightly unkempt look. The sprawling park is mostly rolling lawns, but also embraces a lake, cycle paths, children's play areas and an intriguing design museum. The lack of a museum café in the Castello Sforzesco means that it's best to have lunch in the Triennale design museum (see page 110) or to graze just outside the park at Van Bol & Feste, who also provide tasty picnic treats (see page 110).

CASTELLO SFORZESCO

Castello Sforzesco ❼ was originally built in 1360–70 by Galeazzo II Visconti, and extended by his successor, Gian Galeazzo. Framed by a tower in each of its four corners, this was a vast, oppressive fortification with drawbridges over a deep moat, connecting to an outer wall (the Ghirlanda). In 1447 the Visconti fell from power and the populace tore

Torre del Filarete

down the fortifications, using the old stones to pay off debts and restore the old town walls.

Under the next ruling dynasty, the Sforza, the castle was transformed into the Corte Ducale, a sumptuous ducal residence. Beside it they constructed the **Cortile della Rocchetta** – a fort within a fort – and added the lofty Torre di Bona (Bona Tower). During this golden age in Milan's history, leading literati, artists and musicians were summoned to the court. In the late 15th century, Leonard da Vinci was nominated engineer and painter to the court (see box) and Donato Bramante was enlisted as a court architect and painter.

In 1497 Louis XII of France claimed his right to the duchy of Milan, and the last Sforza fled into exile. Under the Spaniards the castle was used purely for military purposes, and after the French attacked the city in 1733 it fell into decline. Napoleon restored it for military use, creating a parade ground, transforming the ducal chapel into stables and the ducal apartments into dormitories.

Plans to demolish the castle in the late 19th century were thwarted by the architect Luca Beltrami, who, in 1893–1904, restored its aspect as a Renaissance fortress and created a major museum complex within its walls.

Heralding the castle from the city side is an eye-catching fountain, a reconstruction of the Fascistic original. The Milanese nicknamed the fountain *'tort de' spus'*, dialect for 'wedding cake'. Start your visit at the **Torre del Filarete** (Filarete Tower), facing the city. Built in 1452 by the Florentine Antonio Averlino, the tower collapsed when gunpowder stored here exploded in 1521, so this is an early 20th-century copy. The gateway leads into the huge courtyard, the Piazza d'Armi, and from here to the Corte Ducale, where the Sforza dynasty resided.

CASTLE MUSEUMS

The **castle museums** (www.milanocastello.it; Tue–Sun 9am–5.30pm; book online for tours of the towers) appeal to diverse tastes but the Museum of Ancient Art triumphs, with its Michelangelo masterpiece, followed by the Pinacoteca (Art Gallery), which has a fine collection of Venetian Old Masters.

The **Museo d'Arte Antica** (Museum of Ancient Art) on the ground floor of the Corte Ducale displays an extensive sculpture collection, from early Christian to medieval and Renaissance works. Highlights include a late Roman sarcophagus, Romanesque sculpture and Bonino da Campione's equestrian funerary monument to Bernabò Visconti, who ruled Milan from 1354–85. The vaulted Sale delle Asse (Room 8) is frescoed with entwined laurel

Cooling off in Castello Sforzesco's 'wedding cake' fountain

Arco della Pace

branches, designed by Leonardo da Vinci and executed by pupils – though much restored. Among the highlights is Agostini Busto's lifelike Tomb of Gaston de Foix, the young commander of the French Army who died heroically at Ravenna in 1512.

Opened in May 2015, the **Pietà Rondanini Museum** (tel: 02 884 63703; http://rondanini.milanocastello.it; Tue–Sun 9am–5.30pm) is dedicated exclusively to Michelangelo's master-piece – *Rondanini Pietà* (1554–64). This evocative sculptural group was left unfinished – Michelangelo was working on it for nine years and until days before his death (aged 88). The work went through at least two different stages, as revealed by remnants from the original, notably Christ's hanging right arm. The museum is located inside the ancient *Ospedale Spagnolo* (Spanish Hospital) which previously had been closed to the public.

The upper floor in the Ducal Court houses the **Pinacoteca** (Art Gallery), which displays Lombard and Venetian art, including works by Mantegna, Giovanni Bellini and Tintoretto. The other, more specialist, collections are devoted to furniture, musical instruments, the applied arts (including precious tapestries) and an archaeological collection of Egyptian and prehistoric works.

PARCO SEMPIONE

Stretching out behind the Castello Sforzesco is the revamped **Parco Sempione** ❽. Once the haunt of dodgy characters and drug addicts, it is now an inviting park, complete with landscaped gardens, a vibrant design museum with an equally exciting restaurant, and even complimentary Wi-fi in the park. The Sforza's original hunting ground here was six times the size of the present park. Napoleon had grand plans to build a monumental city centred on the park, but only got as far as the Arena and the **Arco della Pace** (Arch of Peace).

Built at the northwest end of the park, this classical triumphal arch marked the start of the route to the Simplon Pass and France. It was originally named the Arch of Victories and decorated with bas-reliefs commemorating Napoleonic conquests, but work stopped when the French defeat at Waterloo in 1815. It was another 24 years before it was completed. The opportunistic Austrian

Savings

A three-day Tourist Museum Card can be bought online for €12 from www.comune.milano.it/cultura and includes free entry to all civic museums in Milan, including those in Sforza Castle. Another option is the MilanoCard, which includes free public transport and free entry or discounts at more than 500 Milan tourist attractions and over 20 museums, which can be purchased at www.milano card.it. 24, 48 and 72 hour cards are available and cost €7, €13 and €19 respectively.

Cimitero Monumentale's elaborate entrance house

emperor Francis I switched the Chariot of Peace round on top of the arch to face the centre of Milan (rather than Paris), altered the bas-reliefs and renamed the monument Arch of Peace in commemoration of the 1815 Congress of Vienna.

On the eastern side of the park, the **Arena Civica**, a Roman-style amphitheatre, was the venue for chariot races, festivities and even mock naval battles, using water from the canals. Seating 30,000, it is used today as a sports stadium, and as a venue for concerts and civil weddings.

The **Triennale**, on the western side of the park, opened in 1932 as a museum for exhibitions and the decorative arts but has been reborn as the **Triennale Design Museum** (www.triennale.org; Tue–Sun 10.30am–8.30pm). This is the first museum in Italy devoted solely to design. For anyone lukewarm about design, the museum is still engaging, with a playful space and a compact permanent collection ranging from the post-war period to the present day. This is matched by hit-and-miss design exhibitions. The Triennale café and restaurant is predictably trendy and serves interesting food to a critical arts crowd (see page 110).

Close to the Triennale, the metallic **Torre Branca** is Milan's answer to the Eiffel Tower (summer Tue 3–7pm and 8.30pm–midnight, Wed 10.30am–12.30pm, 3–7pm and 8.30pm–midnight, Thu–Fri 3–7pm and 8.30pm–midnight, Sat–Sun 10.30am–7.30pm and 8.30pm–midnight; winter Wed 10.30am–12.30pm and 4–6.30pm, Sat 10.30am–1pm, 3–6.30pm and 8.30pm–midnight, Sun 10.30am–7pm; closed in bad weather). Designed in 1933 by the Milanese architect Giò Ponti as part of the Triennale exhibition, the tower has a lift that whisks you up 108m (354ft) for a panorama of the city. Back at the bottom, if suitably dressed, consider a cocktail in the flashy Just Cavalli Café, or supper in the equally kitsch restaurant, both owned by rock royalty's favourite fashion designer, Roberto Cavalli.

CIMITERO MONUMENTALE

Flamboyant designer tombs and funerary monuments provide a fascinating open-air gallery at Milan's **Cimitero Monumentale** ❾ (Piazzale Cimitero Monumentale; Tue–Sun 8am–6pm). The cemetery lies north of Parco Sempione, close to Stazione Porta Garibaldi. Dating from 1866, it is full of Art Nouveau, neoclassical and modern monuments. The focal point is the Famae Aedes (House of Fame), the resting place of illustrious Italians such as the conductor Arturo Toscanini and the novelist Alessandro Manzoni.

THE BRERA

A short stroll from La Scala down Via Verdi brings you to the Brera, a chic quarter which has not sold its soul. Today, this picturesque patch of cobbled streets, cosy inns, discreet boutiques and fashionable

Restaurant options

Pulsating new neighbourhoods are springing up all around this area, but for now the most civilised dining options lie just east, in Corso Como 10, or Acanto on Piazza della Repubblica (see page 111).

nightspots is a reassuring choice for Milanese in search of a mellow mood. The quirky art galleries and indie boutiques still provide a hint of Bohemia. After dark this is a lively quarter. Dozens of new haunts have sprung up, from arty bars and late-night ice-cream parlours to designer cafés where you can sip an *aperitivo* alfresco while tucking into new-wave *stuzzichini* (nibbles). Yet the evocation of 'old Milan' survives, despite the fusion food, backchatting African bag-sellers and eccentric fortune-tellers who line Via Fiori Chiari after dark.

Statue of Napoleon at Pinacoteca di Brera

PINACOTECA DI BRERA

This quarter is also home to the Accademia di Belle Arti (Academy of Fine Arts) and the **Pinacoteca di Brera** ❿ (Brera Art Gallery, Via Brera 28; http://pinacoteca brera.org; Tue–Sun 8.30am– 7.15pm, until 10.15pm on Thu; book online on www. vivaticket.it or tel: 02 9280 0361). Set in Palazzo Brera, Milan's showcase museum possesses one of the finest collections of Italian masterpieces. The Jesuits ran a college, library and observatory here, but when the Order was disbanded in 1772, Empress Maria Theresa of Austria established the Accademia di Belle Arti.

From this Academy, a core collection was enriched with works of art from northern Italian churches and convents suppressed by Napoleon. Added to the collection were representative paintings from foreign art movements.

A bronze statue of Napoleon dressed as a Roman hero greets you as you enter the inner courtyard, where a double stairway leads up to the art galleries.

Francesco Hayez's The Kiss

The collection spans some six centuries, and the rooms are roughly chronological.

The following is a selection of the masterpieces on display. *The Dead Christ* (*c.*1500) by Mantegna (Room VI) demonstrates the artist's controlled style and mastery of dramatic foreshortening. It was painted at the end of his life and probably intended for his own tomb in the church of Sant'Andrea in Mantua. In the same room are two notable works by his brother-in-law, Giovanni Bellini: the *Pietà* and a beautiful *Madonna and Child*, painted when he was nearly 80. Room VII has portraits by some of the great Venetian masters; Room VIII has the huge detailed depiction of *St Mark Preaching in Alexandria* begun by Gentile Bellini in 1504 and completed after his death by his brother Giovanni in 1507.

Room IX's *Discovery of the Body of St Mark* (1565) by Tintoretto shows the artist's mastery of perspective and theatrical effects of light and movement. In the same room,

Artwork by Polish sculptor, Igor Mitoraj, outside the church of Santa Maria del Carmine

Veronese's *Feast in the House of Simon* (1570) was originally commissioned as *The Last Supper*, but the hedonistic detail was not appreciated and Veronese found himself before the Inquisition. Room X jumps to the 20th century, with the Jesi private collection of paintings and sculpture, including works by Modigliani, Picasso and Braque. In Room XIX the *Madonna of the Rose Garden*, by the prolific Milanese painter, Bernardino Luini, shows the influence of Leonardo da Vinci in his subjects' faces and expressions.

Room XXIV has the two most celebrated works in the collection: *The Montefeltro Altarpiece* (1472–4) by Piero della Francesca was painted for his patron, Duke Federico da Montefeltro, who is shown kneeling – the ostrich egg dangling above the Madonna is a famous detail, giving depth to the scene as well as symbolic value (of the Immaculate Conception); and Raphael's serene *Marriage of the Virgin* (1504) evokes a sense of harmony between the architecture and the natural world. In Room XXIX *Supper at Emmaus* (1606) by Caravaggio is a fine example of the artist's realism and chiaroscuro; Francesco Hayez's *The Kiss* (1859) in Room XXXVII became a symbol of 19th-century romantic painting.

CHURCHES AND CAFÉS OF THE BRERA

Part of the charm of the Brera lies in the serendipity of galleries, churches and cafés, all tightly packed into a small, cobblestoned corner of 'old Milan'. The loveliest church in the Brera is the Romanesque basilica of **San Simpliciano** (Piazza San Simpliciano; www.sansimpliciano.it; daily 7am–noon, 3–7pm). Thought to have been founded by Sant'Ambrogio in the 4th century, it was reconstructed 800 years later but – apart from the apse and facade, added in 1870 – retains its original Early Christian form. The apse has a fresco of *The Coronation of the Virgin* by the Lombard Renaissance painter Il Bergognone.

San Marco (Piazza San Marco; daily 7.30am–1pm, 4–7.15pm) is the largest church after the Duomo. It was dedicated to St Mark, patron saint of Venice, in gratitude to the Venetians for their part in the Lombard League, which saw off Frederick Barbarossa, the Holy Roman Emperor, when he laid siege to the city in 1162. Apart from the portal and tower, little is left of the original Gothic structure: a Baroque interior with nine decorated chapels lies behind a neo-Gothic facade.

Overlooking the cobbled Piazza del Carmine, **Santa Maria del Carmine** (daily 8am–6.30pm; free) was rebuilt in Gothic style in 1456 and given a mock Gothic-Lombard facade in 1880. The Baroque interior is a backdrop for art by Camillo Procaccini and Fiammenghino. In the adjoining cloister are remains of Roman and medieval funerary sculptures.

Santa Maria del Carmine

As for the cafés part of the equation, on the same square is the cool Marc Jacobs Café, but Cinc (on Via Formentini), has far more character while the cafés and restaurants on Via Fiori Chiari are more fun, at least after sunset (see page 93).

FASHION DISTRICT – NORTHEAST OF THE DUOMO

For most visitors to Milan the main draw in this district is the chic 'Fashion Quadrangle', known as the Quadrilatero d'Oro or the Quadrilatero della Moda. But if fashion leaves you cold, even as a spectator sport, escape to three highly individualistic art collections, all of which provide insight into Milanese life and the minds of the high society patrons behind these quirky collections. The two best museums are the Museo Poldi Pezzoli and the Museo Bagatti Valsecchi, which appeal to different sensibilities but are equally deserving of attention. Further north, the Giardini Pubblici (Public Gardens) make a welcome break from pounding the city streets.

QUADRILATERO D'ORO

Fashionistas will make a beeline for the cutting-edge collections in this celebrated shopping quarter. Easily covered on foot, it is a compact, surprisingly discreet area, bordered by Via Monte Napoleone (familiarly known as Montenapo), Via Manzoni, Via Spiga and Via Sant'Andrea. All the big names are here, from Armani and Prada to Versace and Dolce & Gabbana. Prices are sky-high, but it's worth coming just to window-shop at the gallery-like boutiques – and see the impeccably clad Milanese who frequent them. Stores range from chic little shops in beautifully preserved *palazzi* to large and modern fashion emporia. What's more, you can now find discount stores

In the Quadrilatero d'Oro

even in the fashion district, with Kilo Fascion currently the best (see page 87).

Consider taking a break from shopping at highbrow Café Cova at Via Monte Napoleone 8, which attracts both sweet-toothed Milanese matrons and the fashion crowd. Alternatively, slip into Café Conti at No. 19 for an aperitif, or join the fashionistas at the Armani café. If you're allergic to fashion victims, then Bice is the best upmarket *trattoria* in the area (see page 112).

MUSEO BAGATTI VALSECCHI

In and around the Quadrilatero d'Oro are a clutch of delightful 'historic house museums' (www.casemuseo milano.it) that dispel any notion of Milan as an impersonal metropolis. The most intimate is the **Museo Bagatti Valsecchi** ⓫ (Via Gèsu 5; www.museobagattivalsecchi.org; Tue–Sun 1–5.45pm), a fascinating museum housed within a neo-Renaissance palace. Brothers Fausto and Giuseppe

Valsecchi, following the *fin-de-siècle* fashion for collecting in 1876–95, transformed two palaces into an authentic evocation of the Renaissance. The dilettante brothers lived here in private apartments but shared the drawing room, dining room and gallery of armour. Every work of art, chest or tapestry is either an original Renaissance piece or a perfect copy. Rooms have been lavishly decorated with painted ceilings, frescoes and elaborate fireplaces, while 19th-century necessities such as the bathtub are cleverly masked in a Renaissance-style marble niche.

GRAND HOTEL ET DE MILAN

The Grand Hotel et de Milan at Via Manzoni 29 opened in 1863 as the Albergo di Milano. Towards the end of the 19th century, it was the only hotel in the city that offered post and telegraph services, and hence was popular with diplomats and businessmen. A stone's throw from La Scala, it has long been a favourite among musicians and artists. The Italian composer Giuseppe Verdi (1813–1901) stayed here from 1872 until his death, with breaks at his country residence in Sant'Agata, near Parma.

After an absence of 24 years from La Scala, Verdi made his comeback with a performance of *Otello* in 1887. Afterwards, the Milanese hailed the composer, gathering below his balcony at the hotel, and he sang an encore of the opera's arias with the tenor Tamagno. In the last years of Verdi's life, frequent bulletins about his health were posted in the hotel lobby, and whenever he was seriously ill crowds would gather outside.

During his dying hours the Via Manzoni was laid out with straw to muffle the clatter of the carriages. Other eminent guests at the hotel include kings, emperors, presidents, famous artists and film stars.

MUSEO POLDI PEZZOLI

Elegant Via Manzoni is lined by noble *palazzi*, but another unmissable historic home is No. 12, the **Museo Poldi Pezzoli** ⑫ (www.museo poldipezzoli.it; Wed–Mon 10am–6pm). Aristocrat Gian Giacomo Poldi Pezzoli certainly had good taste – his palace contains an exquisite collection of art, antiques and curios. Helped by an inheritance and a coterie of craftsmen, connoisseurs and artists, Poldi Pezzoli

Portrait of a Young Woman at Museo Poldi Pezzoli

restored the palace and filled it with his priceless treasures. He stipulated that on his death the building and contents should be accessible to the public.

The museum opened in 1881, with the Arms and Armoury (Poldi Pezzoli's great passion) forming the core collection. To this was added 15th–18th-century Italian paintings, sculpture, Persian carpets, porcelain and Murano glass. The highlights are paintings by Renaissance masters in the Salone Dorato (Golden Salon), such as Mantegna's *Portrait of a Man* and *Madonna and Child*, Piero della Francesca's *Deposition and St Nicholas of Tolentino* and Botticelli's *Madonna and Child*. But the local citizens' favourite painting is the enchanting *Portrait of a Young Woman* by Pollaiuolo (1441–96), which is now the museum's emblem.

Nearby, No. 10 Via Manzoni is home to the **Galleria d'Italia** (www.gallerieditalia.com; Tue–Sun 9.30am–7.30pm), housed in adjoining neoclassical palaces. Italian banks often own

Planetario 'Ulrico Hoepli' in the Giardini Pubblici

remarkable art collections and these are no exception. Together, Fondazione Cariplo and Intesa Sanpaolo showcase 19th-century art, much of it featuring Milan, by artists ranging from Canova to Hayez, Boldoni and Boccioni.

For a change of scene, stroll in the pedestrian district nearby, from the touristy, café-lined **Corso Vittorio Emanuele II** to **Galleria del Corso**, the trendy shopping gallery. Known as the Excelsior, it is home to designer fripperies as well as to Eat's, an inviting café, bistro and food hall (see page 108). Fortified by a designer coffee, head north to **Villa Necchi Campiglio** on Via Mozart (www.casemuseo milano.it; Wed–Sun 10am–6pm) and a slice of Modernist Milan. In 1932 the socialite Necchi sisters enlisted local architect Piero Portaluppi to build them a coolly glamorous villa in the city centre. The sisters plumped for the Rationalist architect responsible for much of Milan's cityscape and Portaluppi did them proud. The sisters were keen collectors and the villa remains a testament to the times, from glamorous 1930s furnishings to the evocative gardens, decadent pool and peaceful café (see page 112).

GIARDINI PUBBLICI

In this leafy, privileged district, Corso Venezia leads north to the **Giardini Pubblici** ⓭ (Public Gardens). These were originally designed by Piermarini in 1782, then revamped in romantic 'English style'. Close by is the neoclassical Villa Reale (Royal Villa), once the residence of Napoleon but now home to a fittingly French art collection. The **Galleria d'Arte Moderna** is confusingly also known as the **Museo dell'Ottocento** (Museum of the 19th Century; www. gam-milano.com; Tue–Sun 9am–5.30pm), which is more accurate. The grandiose rooms make a fine frame for the succession of dreamy canvases by Renoir, Millet and Courbet. The 20th-century art has mostly moved to the Museo del Novecento (see page 36).The villa gardens, with lawns, a fish-filled lake and Doric temple are more secluded than the Giardini Pubblici.

The neighbouring **PAC** or **Padiglione d'Arte Contemporanea** (Pavilion of Contemporary Art; www.pacmilano.it; Tue–Sun 9.30am–7.30pm, until 10.30pm on Thu) is the main exhibition space for contemporary art. Devastated by a Mafia car bomb in 1993, the pavilion was reconstructed according to its original design. The **Museo Civico di Storia Naturale** (Natural History Museum; Corso Venezia 55; www.comune.milano.it; Tue–Sun 9am–5.30pm) is the biggest of its kind in Italy. It has reconstructions of dinosaurs and striking dioramas as well as specialist sections such as geology, mineralogy, palaeontology and entomology.

The nearby **Planetario 'Ulrico Hoepli'** (Ulrico Hoepli Planetarium; Corso Venezia 57; tel: 02 8846 3340; variable times) shows projections of the night sky on a fairly regular basis.

WEST OF THE CENTRE

Leonardo's *Last Supper* is the star attraction of this district, an area that is also home to Sant'Ambrogio, the city's most beguiling church, and the one most treasured by the Milanese. This was a monastic district in medieval times but today is the preserve of the bourgeoisie. The discreet charm of the bourgeoisie seeps into a residential district of secret courtyards, severe mansions and smart tearooms. The Corso Magenta, arguably Milan's most elegant boulevard, links a series of museums.

THE LAST SUPPER

In *A Traveller in Italy* (1964) H.V. Morton commented that 'there can be few cities in the world, in which you can give the title of a great picture as a topographical direction'. He was referring to Leonardo da Vinci's *The Last Supper (Il Cenacolo)* and the

VISITING THE LAST SUPPER

Tickets for *The Last Supper* can only be booked in advance, either via the call centre (tel: (+39) 02 9280 0360; Mon–Fri 9am–6pm, Sat 9am–2pm) or, more speedily, online at www.vivaticket.it. If tickets are unavailable, or you want more on Leonardo, take a dedicated *Last Supper* tour, bookable through the tourist office, which includes the painting, monastic church and even a tour of 'Leonardo's Milan'. The painting is in the refectory of the Convent of Santa Maria delle Grazie (Piazza Santa Maria delle Grazie; Tue–Sun 8.15am–6.45pm; metro Cadorna/Conciliazione. A maximum of 25 visitors at a time can pass through three acclimatisation and de-polluting chambers before gaining access, and visits are restricted to 15 minutes. Audio-guides are available, as are guided tours in English, at 9.30am and 3.30pm.

Leonardo da Vinci's The Last Supper

fact that the name of the painting is all he had to say to a Milan taxi driver to get him there. Visitor numbers saw a meteoric rise after the success of *The Da Vinci Code* – both Dan Brown's best-selling novel and the film that followed. This means tickets need to be booked weeks in advance (see box).

Commissioned in 1495 by Ludovico il Moro for the Dominican convent of Santa Maria delle Grazie, *The Last Supper* covers the whole width of the refectory north wall. It is a compelling mural, and despite heavy restoration over the centuries, makes for a moving experience. A masterpiece of psychological insight, the work shows the emotional reactions on the faces of the Apostles at the split second they hear Christ's announcement that one of them is about to betray him. Their expressions of amazement and disbelief, and the motion depicted by their faces and gestures, contrast with the divine stillness of the central figure of Christ. The only figure to recoil and the only one whose face is not in the light is Judas, the third figure to the left of Christ.

Santa Maria della Grazie

Restoration works, good and bad, have been hampered by Leonardo's experimental technique in painting in *tempera forte*, rather than *fresco* – he applied the paint to dry plaster rather than applying it quickly to a wet surface. This gave him more time to complete the work, but meant that the moisture caused the paint to flake. On completion in 1498, the work drew high praise, but even in Leonardo's lifetime it had begun to disintegrate. When the art historian Vasari saw it a generation later he described it as 'a dazzling blotch'. Reworked in the 18th century, the painting was then badly damaged during the Napoleonic regime when the premises became a stable and the wall was used for target practice. In the following century, heavy-handed restorers managed to peel off an entire layer. Miraculously, the work survived the bombs that fell on the building in 1943. A painstakingly slow restoration process took place in 1978–99, giving rise to major controversy in the art world. Many experts consider the restored colours far too bright.

On the facing wall, *The Crucifixion* (1495) by Donato da Montorfano gets short shrift, especially as time in the refectory is restricted to 15 minutes. But this is also of interest to Leonardo fans, for he added the (now faded) portraits of Ludovico il Moro, the Sforza ruler, with his wife Beatrice and their children, to the painting.

SANTA MARIA DELLE GRAZIE

Such is the fame of *The Last Supper* that the church of **Santa Maria delle Grazie** ⑭ (Mon–Fri 7am–noon, 3–7pm, Sat–Sun 7.15am–12.15pm, 3.30–9pm) in which it sits is often overlooked. This lovely convent church has a superb brick-and-terracotta exterior, a grandiose dome and delightful cloisters. The church was built in Gothic style, but shortly afterwards Ludovico il Moro commissioned Bramante to demolish the chancel and rebuild it as a Renaissance mausoleum for himself and his wife, Beatrice d'Este. His plans for further building were dashed by the French occupation in 1499, and so the interior feels like two different churches: Solari's original with richly decorated arches and vaults, and beyond it Bramante's pure, perfect and simple Renaissance cube, with a massive dome.

SCIENCE MUSEUM

Leonardo's Vitruvian Man drawing

For further proof of Leonardo's genius visit the **Museo della Scienza e della Tecnologia Leonardo da Vinci** ⑮ (Museum of Science and Technology; Via San Vittore 21; www.museoscienza.org; Tue–Sun 10am–6pm, until 7pm on Sat–Sun), south of Santa Maria delle Grazie.

Sculpture in Civico Museo Archeologico

This is a daunting museum, set within the cloistered former monastery of St Vittore. Supported by interactive labs, the array of exhibits cover all the sciences, including subjects as diverse as watch-making, hammer-forging, locomotion and the workings of the internet. A star attraction is the Enrico Toti submarine (separate charge), which was built in 1967 to track Soviet submarines in the Mediterranean. In 2005 it was towed from Sicily, along the Adriatic up the River Po to Cremona, carted on wheels, and over several nights inched its way through the streets of Milan to the museum. Viewing numbers are limited to six at a time.

On the first floor the collection of models demonstrates the genius of Leonardo's inventions. His technical drawings are reproduced along with modern interpretative drawings and descriptions. Leonardo never intended his designs to be used for construction plans, and in some cases the machines don't work. Not that this detracts from their appeal – some of the machines were developed later with success.

MUSEO ARCHEOLOGICO AND SAN MAURIZIO

On the same street as Santa Maria delle Grazie, as you head towards the centre, is the **Civico Museo Archeologico** ⑯ (Museum of Archaeology; Corso Magenta 15; www.comune.milano.it; Tue–Sun 9am–5.30pm). Set among the cloisters and ruins of the Gothic Monastero Maggiore, formerly Milan's largest convent, the museum houses Roman sculpture, mosaics, ceramics and glassware. Star exhibits are the gilded silver Parabiago Plate, with engravings of the goddess Cybele, and the Coppa Trivulzio, an emerald-green glass goblet, both dating from the 4th century. Further sections are devoted to Greek, Etruscan, Indian and medieval collections. Behind the museum lie ruins of a 24-sided Roman tower and a segment of the old town wall.

Beside the Archaeological Museum, and built for the Benedictine nuns from the Monastero Maggiore, is the 16th-century church of **San Maurizio** (Tue–Sat 9.30am–5.30pm). The sober grey-stone facade on the street belies the vivid, restored interior with its riot of frescoes. The nuns were

A Fresco in the San Maurizio church

cut off from the congregation by a partition, and to the right of the altar you can see the tiny opening through which they received Holy Communion. The frescoes are mostly the work of the Lombard artist, Bernardino Luini, as are the lunettes on either side of the altar, which depict his patrons, Alessandro Bentivoglio, prince of Bologna, and his wife Ippolita Sforza.

BASILICA DI SANT'AMBROGIO

Beyond is the city's loveliest church, **Sant'Ambrogio** ⑰ (Piazza Sant'Ambrogio; www.basilicasantambrogio.it; Mon–Sat 10am–noon, 2.30–6pm, Sun 3–5pm). This graceful red-brick church was founded in the 4th century by Ambrogio (St Ambrose), the city's bishop and future patron saint (see page 17). The church you see today – a fine Romanesque basilica flanked by two campaniles – dates from the 9th–12th centuries and became the prototype for Lombard-Romanesque basilicas. In front of it, the perfectly preserved, porticoed **atrium** was built as a shelter for pilgrims. The composite columns have finely carved capitals, with lively sculptures of mythical creatures and Christian symbols.

Inside is the beautifully carved Byzantine-Romanesque **pulpit**, standing over a 4th-century Palaeochristian sarcophagus. Below the 9th-century ciborium (canopy) is the jewel-encrusted gold and silver **altarpiece** (835), a masterpiece by the German goldsmith Volvinio. Panels on the front depict scenes from the *Life of Christ*, and on the back the *Life of Sant'Ambrogio*. To the right of the sacristy the **Cappella di San Vittore in Ciel d'Oro** (Chapel of St Victor in the Sky of Gold) is decorated by splendid 5th-century mosaics, depicting Sant'Ambrogio and other saints. In the crypt below the presbytery the saint's

Basilica di Sant'Ambrogio

Stroll along the towpaths in the Navigli quarter

remains share a silver-and-crystal urn with those of the martyred Roman soldiers Gervasius and Protasius.

THE SOUTH: THE CANAL QUARTER AND THE TICINESE

It is hard to believe that landlocked Milan was once an important port with a major network of canals. Trade on the waterways ceased in the late 1970s, and the Navigli (canal quarter) has been undergoing a transformation ever since. Galleries, inns and bars proliferate along the towpaths, and the area is now a buzzing nightlife centre, though generally sleepy by day. Between the Duomo and the Navigli lie two of Milan's oldest and finest churches, San Lorenzo and Sant'Eustorgio. Further east, the now traffic-clogged Corso di Porta Romana was the ancient road to Rome.

THE NAVIGLI

The Navigli were key navigable waterways, linking Milan to the River Ticino, which descends from Switzerland via

Lake Maggiore to Pavia and, via the Po, to the sea. Work on the **Naviglio Grande** (Grand Canal) started in 1177, and the waterway was initially used by horse- and oxen-drawn barges. The first 30km (19 miles) took half a century to construct and involved hundreds of men with shovels and axes. They finally reached Milan in 1272, but works came to a standstill when the Milanese opposed the project, particularly the clergy, who were charged a new tax to help finance it.

In 1359, under Galeazzo II Visconti, excavations began on the **Naviglio Pavese,** the canal to Pavia whose main function was to irrigate the great park surrounding the Visconti castle at Pavia. Under his successor, Gian Galeazzo Visconti, the foundation stone of Milan's Duomo was laid (1386), and the canals were then used to ship huge blocks of marble from the Candoglia quarries near Lake Maggiore to Milan. Barges travelled along the Ticino River to the Naviglio Grande and Milan's city dockyard. Leonardo da Vinci was fascinated by waterways, and one of his many tasks during his employment in the court of Ludovico il Moro, of the Sforza dynasty, was to suggest improvements to the canal network. In the Biblioteca Ambrosiana, the *Codex Atlanticus* shows Leonardo's scientific bent, revealing his schemes for waterways and canal sluice gates, including a double-door closing mechanism and a sluice-gate system that is still in use today.

Following the Sforza dynasty, long periods of neglect were brought about by foreign rule, wars, pestilence and earthquakes. In 1809, under Napoleon, the

Canal tours

Navigli Lombardi run one-hour canal cruises from April to September. Boats run regularly from Alzaia Naviglio Grande 4; tel: 02 667 9131; www.navigliolombardi.it (in Italian only).

first section of the Naviglio Pavese became navigable, and in 1816, after 600 years, the 50km (30 miles) of the Naviglio Grande were finally completed. Added to the 101km (63 miles) of other canals and 81km (50 miles) of navigable river reaches, this formed a waterway network of 232km (145 miles). Between 1830 and the end of the century, an annual average of 8,300 barges, transporting 350,000 tonnes of trade, arrived at the dockyard of Porta Ticinese.

The weekly Fiera di Senigallia flea market

Canal traffic suffered with competition from railways in the 19th century, but saw a brief surge of activity during the post-war building boom. But competition from road transport finally led to the demise of canal trade; the waterways were filled in, and the last barge delivered its shipment of sand in 1979. Nowadays, the only water transport comes in the form of pleasure cruises along the few surviving canals (see box).

THE NAVIGLI TODAY

The **Porta Ticinese** ⓲ on Piazzale XXIV Maggio heralds the Navigli quarter. This original gateway, which formed part of the 12th-century city walls, was replaced in 1804 by the present-day monumental arch. It stands isolated in the square, surrounded by traffic.

Formerly the most insalubrious quarter of the city, the Navigli has been regenerated over the last few decades, and now has a mix of working-class and upwardly mobile residents. The industrial sites and tenement blocks have been reincarnated as desirable designer apartments, towpaths are lined with galleries, craft workshops and quirky shops, giving it a faintly bohemian air, and a host of bars, jazz clubs and restaurants have moved in. So too have festivals, fairs and markets. Apart from the weekly flea market, the huge Mercatone dell'Antiquariato is held on the last Sunday of the month from September to June, with around 400 antique dealers spreading their wares along the canal banks.

The **Darsena** (dockyard), built in 1603, used to be the hub of the Navigli quarter, where barges docked to offload their cargo. What used to be a neglected stretch of murky water was regenerated, at a cost of nearly €20 million, before Expo 2015 to become a trendy, pedestrianised area. The harbour is once again navigable and a small section of the Ticinello Canal, which was buried in the 1930s, has been reopened. The quarter comes alive on Saturdays when the stalls of the Fiera di Senigallia flea market spread out along **Ripa di Porta Ticinese**, further up the **Naviglio Grande Canal**.

Most of the Navigli nightlife takes place along the two towpaths running either side of the Naviglio Grande: the Ripa di Porta Ticinese and the **Alzaia Naviglio Grande**. But recently there has been a shift, with the upper end of Alzaia Naviglio Grande, closest to the Darsena,

Route canal

The Cerchia di Navigli was the circle of navigable canals surrounding the city. In 1930, when canal trade was on the decline, the waterways were filled in to become Milan's traffic-clogged ring road. But plans are afoot to restore the waterways to something of their former splendour.

Naviglio Grande (Grand Canal)

attracting a more sophisticated set, partly because of the emergence of the **Zona Tortona design district** on the far side of **Porta Genova station**. As a result, this upper stretch is lined with attractive restaurants and even a boutique hotel (see page 141). It also features the excellent **Museum of Cultures** (MUDEC; Mon 2.30–7.30pm, Tue–Sun 9.30am–7.30pm, till 10.30pm Thu and Sun), which opened in 2015 and is located in a splendid building designed by architect David Chipperfield on the grounds of the former Ansaldo factory. Besides its many ethnographic collections, this inter-disciplinary centre offers cultural activities, workshops and hosts temporary exhibitions. There are also restaurants, a library, an auditorium, lecture rooms and the Mudec Junior area, where children aged 4–11 can learn about cultures from around the world in an informative yet innovative way. Fashion buffs must visit the nearby **Armani Silos** (www.armanisilos.com; Wed–Sun 11am–7pm, until 9pm Thu and Sat) exhibition centre. Opened in 2015 to mark the designer's

Lavish marble sarcophagus in the Cappella Portinari

40 years in fashion, the centre displays some of his most iconic creations, including one of Richard Gere's suits worn by the actor in *American Gigolo*.

By the same token, younger, funkier nightlife is moving towards the other significant canal, the **Alzaia Naviglio Pavese**. Barges have been converted into bars and boisterous restaurants, as well as nightclubs, jazz clubs and *aperitivo* bars that come and go. More of a fixture are the host of *trattorie* with tables set out along the banks of the canals. If you come in the daytime, though, it can be distinctly lifeless beyond the chic stretch of the Alzaia Naviglio Grande. The prettiest corner is, typically, at the chic end of the Alzaia Naviglio Grande. Known as the **Vicolo del Lavandai** (Laundry Lane), it is named after the old wash-houses, which retain their wooden roofs and the stone slabs where the laundry was scrubbed.

THE TICINESE DISTRICT

North of the Navigli lies the funky **Porta Ticinese district**. Once a dormitory suburb for Milanese factory workers, it is now a vibrant young designer district as well as being home to several significant churches. The Corso di Porta Ticinese has a friendly, alternative feel, helped by a mix of everyday and bohemian shops, and enlivened by the clatter of trams running close by.

The two great basilicas of the Ticinese quarter lie just east of the main Corso di Porta Ticinese. **Sant'Eustorgio ⑲** (Piazza Sant'Eustorgio; Mon–Sun 7.45am–6.30pm), distinctive for its lofty bell tower, has Early Christian origins, but was destroyed by Frederick Barbarossa in 1162 and rebuilt over several centuries. Highlights of the church are the private Renaissance chapels, and most notably the beautiful little **Cappella Portinari** (1462–6), which can only be seen by visiting the Museo di Sant'Eustorgio (daily 10am–6pm; combined ticket with Museo Diocesano, and the Cappella Sant'Aquilino at San Lorenzo, see page 78).

Similar to Brunelleschi's Cappella Pazzi in Florence, this simple chapel was one of the first Renaissance works in the city. Traditionally attributed to the Florentine Michelozzo, it is now believed to have been designed by a Lombard architect working in Tuscan circles. The chapel was commissioned by Pigello Portinari, a Florentine nobleman and agent of the Medici Bank in Milan, to house the relics of St Peter Martyr – as well as his own. St Peter Martyr (Pietro da Verona) was an Inquisitor who persecuted the Cathars, one of whom took revenge and killed him in 1252. His relics lie in the lavishly carved marble sarcophagus (1339), a masterpiece by Giovanni Balduccio from Pisa. The saint's skull is protected in a silver reliquary in the chapel to the left of the altar.

Statue of emperor Constantine outside the church of San Lorenzo Maggiore

Corinthian columns in front of San Lorenzo Maggiore church

Stunning frescoes by the Tuscan artist Vincenzo Foppa decorate the chapel and depict scenes from the *Life of St Peter Martyr* and the *Virgin Mary*.

The basilica was built to house the supposed relics of the Magi. These are contained in a Roman sarcophagus in the Chapel of the Magi in the right-hand transept of the main church. During the annual *Corteo dei Magi* procession on 6 January (Epiphany), the relics are carried with great ceremony from the Duomo to Sant'Eustorgio. Beside Sant'Eustorgio, the **Museo Diocesano** (Corso di Porta Ticinese 95; www.museo diocesano.it; Tue–Sun 10am–6pm) is arrayed on three floors of the Dominican convent and cloisters, and showcases 320 works from Sant'Ambrogio (see page 68) and other churches in the diocese. Unlike many diocesan museums, which are dull and dusty, Milan's has been renovated and feels like a stylish new art gallery. The works date from the 6th to the 19th centuries, and, as well as religious paintings, there are sculptures, chalices and jewellery Don't miss the

Fondi Oro collection – exquisite Tuscan and Umbrian altarpieces, all with a gold background.

A rose-lined path through the **Parco delle Basiliche** (Park of the Basilicas) links Sant'Eustorgio and San Lorenzo. For many centuries public hangings and torture took place here, while tanners' workshops created a foul stench. Today it is a pleasant park, which affords the best views of the **Basilica di San Lorenzo Maggiore ⑳** (Corso di Porta Ticinese 39; www.sanlorenzomaggiore.com; daily 7.30am–12.30pm, 2.30–6.30pm). After the Duomo, this is the second-largest church in the city, distinctive for its huge central dome and the melange of architectural styles. It is also the oldest surviving church in the city, founded in the 4th century as an early Christian church, remodelled in Romanesque form in the 13th century, and reconstructed in the 16th century after the collapse of the dome in 1573. The facade is the newest addition, dating from 1894.

The 16 lofty Corinthian columns on the square in front of the church came from a Roman temple, and were probably erected here as a part of a portico for the original basilica, hence the alternative name for the church, **San Lorenzo alle Colonne**. In front of the church is a 1942 statue of Constantine the Great, who issued the Edict of Milan, granting freedom of religion to Christians in 313, before the church was built.

Emperor Constantine

Inside the church the Early Christian octagonal plan, though remodelled in the 16th century, has essentially been preserved. On the right, the **Cappella Sant'Aquilino** was built as an imperial mausoleum and retains some beautiful 5thcentury niche mosaics. At the altar, an elaborate silver-and-crystal casket contains the remains of Sant'Aquilino, while a small stairway to the left of the altar descends to the imperial-era foundations.

Building material for San Lorenzo was thought to have been salvaged from the nearby Roman Circus and Amphitheatre. Remnants of the latter can be seen at the **Parco Archeologico e Antiquarium Alda Levi** (Archaelogical Park and Antiquarium, entrance at Via de Amicis 17; Tue–Fri 9.30am–6pm, until 4pm on Sat and in winter; free). The remains of this huge four-storey coliseum were discovered during roadworks here in 1931. Within the park, the Antiquarium (Tue–Sat 9.30am–2pm; free) displays architectural finds from the area, and to liven things up, shows excerpts from such films as *Spartacus* and *Gladiator*. One real-life gladiator, Ubricus, died at the age of 22 having fought 13 times here.

Pavia's university is one of Europe's oldest

EXCURSIONS FROM MILAN

With excellent road and rail links, Milan makes a good starting point for excursions in the Lombardy region. The lakes and mountains are surprisingly close. By train you can be in Stresa on Lake Maggiore, Como on Lake Como or Bergamo within an hour.

The following are briefer excursions from Milan. The Abbazia di Chiaravalle and Monza are both on the city outskirts; Pavia and its Certosa are further away but justify a whole day's excursion.

CHIARAVALLE ABBEY

In 1135 French Cistercian monks drained the marshland southeast of Milan, transforming it into rich agricultural land, and built the splendid **Abbazia di Chiaravalle** ㉑ (Chiaravalle Abbey, Via Sant'Arialdo 102, 7km/4 miles southeast of Milan, metro M3 Corvetto, bus No. 77 from Piazza Medaglie d'Oro; www.monasterochiaravalle.it; opening times vary; guided tours Sat and Sun at 3 and 4pm). The founder was St Bernard, who was the Abbot of Clairvaux in France (Chiaravalle in Italian), to which the new abbey was affiliated.

The church was rebuilt in 1150–60, altered over the centuries, and disbanded under Napoleon. A lengthy restoration was completed in the early 1950s, and Cistercian monks finally returned to the abbey. A blend of Lombard Romanesque and French Gothic, the church is notable for its striking terracotta-and-marble campanile, internal Renaissance and Baroque frescoes, and finely carved wooden choir and Gothic cloisters.

PAVIA

The ancient university town of **Pavia** ㉒ lies on the banks of the River Ticino, 36km (22 miles) south of Milan. Long ago it was one of the leading cities in Italy, reaching its zenith between the 6th and 8th centuries as capital of the Lombard kingdom and site of the coronation of the Holy Roman

Emperors. During the 14th century, the city was subdued by the Visconti dynasty of Milan who built the great Certosa di Pavia (Carthusian monastery), the Castello Visconteo (Visconti Castle), and founded the city's university, one of the oldest in Europe, noted for law, science and medicine.

Pavia today is a pleasant town of cobbled streets and squares, Romanesque and Gothic churches, feudal towers and *palazzi*. The enormous 19th-century dome of the Renaissance Duomo dominates the centre. Amadeo, Leonardo and Bramante were among its architects, but today it is a disappointing hotchpotch of styles. The pile of rubble beside it is all that remains of the medieval tower, which collapsed in 1989, killing four people. The town's finest church is the **Basilica di San Michele**, a masterpiece of Lombard-Romanesque. The church witnessed the coronation of kings here during the Middle Ages, the last being Frederick Barbarossa in 1155. The glorious facade, in mellow sandstone, is decorated with fascinating (but sadly faded) friezes of beasts, birds, mermaids and humans; there are more carvings inside on the columns, which are better preserved. The austere **Visconti Castle**, a mere shadow of the former ducal residence, contains the Civic Museum (www.museicivici.pavia.it; Jul–Aug and Dec–Jan Tue–Sun 9am–1.30pm, rest of the year Tue–Sun 10am–5.50pm), with collections of paintings, sculpture and archaeology.

CERTOSA DI PAVIA

The great **Certosa** ㉓ (Carthusian monastery; tel: 0382 936 911; www.certosadipavia.com; May–Sept Tue–Sun 9–11.30am and 2.30–6pm, Oct –Apr until 4.30pm; for guided tours, arrive one hour before closing time; free, donations welcomed) lies north of Pavia, among fields which were the former hunting ground of the Visconti. One of the most decorative and important monuments in Italy, it was founded in 1396 by Gian Galeazzo Visconti as a mausoleum for himself and his family. However, it was not completed for another 200 years. The Carthusian Order was suppressed in 1782, and since then the monastery has had a chequered history, closed for long periods or variously occupied by Cistercian, Carmelite and Carthusian monks. In 1866 it was declared a national monument, and since 1968 a small community of Cistercian monks have occupied the Certosa.

Creating a striking impact as you enter the gateway is the multi-coloured marble facade, encrusted with a proliferation of medallions, bas-reliefs and statues of saints and prophets. The monument marks the transition from late Gothic to Renaissance: the interior is essentially Gothic, created by some of the same architects and artisans who worked on

Encrusted facade of the Certosa

Duomo di San Giovanni, Monza

Milan's Duomo; the lower level of the facade dates from the 15th century, and the plainer upper facade from the first decades of the 16th century.

The soaring interior is a treasure house of Renaissance and Baroque works of art. Outstanding among them are the funerary monument of Ludovico il Moro and his wife Beatrice d'Este, the mausoleum of Gian Galeazzo Visconti, frescoes by Bergognone in the transept, chapels and roof vaults, the marquetry in the choir stalls, the altarpiece by Perugino and the Florentine triptych, made of hippopotamus teeth and other animal bones, in the Old Sacristy. Visits end at the Certosa shop selling the local Carnaroli rice, honey, herbal remedies and liqueurs.

Regular trains and buses link Pavia with Milan. The Certosa, 8km (5 miles) to the north, has its own train station and bus stop, but both are a 1.5km (1-mile) walk from the monument, mostly along a main road, which can be tiring on a hot summer's day.

MONZA

Once an important medieval town and the site of the coronation of many Lombard kings, **Monza** ㉔ today merges with the industrial suburbs of northwest Milan and is best-known for Grand Prix motor-racing. The town has been revamped for Milan's Expo 2015. Even so, Monza's centrepiece remains the Gothic **Duomo di San Giovanni** (Cathedral of St John; www.duomomonza.it), founded by the Lombard queen Theodolinda in 595 and rebuilt from the 13th–14th centuries. The Cappella di Teodolinda (Theodolinda Chapel), frescoed with scenes from the life of the queen, contains her sarcophagus and the gem-studded 'Iron Crown', which was used for the coronation of 34 Lombard kings, from medieval times to the 19th century. The last was Ferdinand I of Austria in 1836, while the penultimate was Napoleon, who assumed the throne of Italy in Milan's cathedral in 1805. Legend has it that a nail within the crown came from Christ's cross – hence the name 'Iron Crown'. Theodolinda-related treasures are kept in the cathedral museum, **Museo Serpero**, including her own bejewelled crown.

Controversially, Monza's Formula One motor-racing still takes place in the 800-hectare (1,977-acre) **Parco di Monza**, as do golf, tennis, swimming, and cycling. This was originally the park of the **Villa Reale** (Royal Villa; www.villareale dimonza.it). This grand neoclassical villa, built in 1777 for Archduke Ferdinand of Austria, was chosen for its location on the route between Milan and Austria. The frescoed, stuccoed royal apartments and the rest of the palace was refurbished ahead of Expo 2015.

Monza is 15km (9 miles) northeast of Milan, and is linked by a regular timetable of trains from Milan's Stazione Garibaldi or Stazione Centrale, with a new metro line scheduled for completion in 2017.

WHAT TO DO

SHOPPING

As the fashion capital of Italy, Milan is a shopper's paradise. Famous for designer boutiques with cutting-edge collections, the city also offers affordable fashion, funky accessories, jewellery and even vintage, as well as design icons, homeware and tempting new food halls.

WHERE TO SHOP

The **Quadrilatero d'Oro** is the designer fashion district *par excellence*. The flagship outlets of Armani, Prada, Dolce & Gabbana, Gucci, Versace and their peers are conveniently concentrated here. This 'Golden Quadrangle', only a short distance from the Duomo, is defined by Via Manzoni, Via Montenapoleone, Via della Spiga and Via Sant'Andrea. The elegant Via Montenapolene – or Monte Napo as the Milanese call it – is the designers' shop window, even if many now have their showrooms in Milan's hippest neighbourhood, the Zona Tortona area (metro Porta Genova).

The Quadrilatero conceals snooty boutiques in beautifully preserved *palazzi* yet also flaunts fashion and lifestyle megastores. **Armani** is the quintessential brand, with a megastore at Via Manzoni 31 which houses Caffè Emporio Armani, Armani Libri (books), and Armani Dolce, in addition to Armani fashion, an Armani Nobu and a new Armani hotel. **Dolce & Gabbana** typify the designers who are following suit, with branded stores, bars, restaurants and barber's.

The centre offers a Milanese mixture. Affordable fashion can be found in the chain stores around the Duomo, but even this area is dotted with designer boutiques, bookstores and bars. For instance, **Trussardi** chose to site their fashion megastore and designer eateries beside La Scala opera house. However,

Admiring the designer shopfronts

the neighbouring **Corso Vittorio Emanuele II** and **Via Dante** are lined with mainstream brands.

A short walk from La Scala lies the atmospheric **Brera**, traditionally the bohemian quarter. These quaintly cobbled streets conceal galleries, antique shops and offbeat boutiques, such as the romantic **Luisa Beccaria** (Via Formentini; tel: 02 863 8071, http://luisabeccaria.it, metro Lanza). The **Navigli canal quarter**, particularly Corso di Porta Ticinese, is the area to head to for younger, hipper, one-off designs, including affordable women's wear at **Dock** (Viale Gorizia 30, metro Porta Genova).

The **Corso Como** area (metro Garibaldi) is perennially fashionable, thanks to the Fiat garage transformed into the concept store known as **Corso Como 10** (www.10corsocomo.com). With a tea garden, lounge bar and restaurant, bookshop, art gallery and music shop, you could spend all day here – and since it has three designer suites above the shop, all night too.

The **Buenos Aires district** (metro Porta Venezia) is the best for affordable young mainstream fashion, including sportswear,

SHOPPING IN COMFORT

Milanese shop assistants can be frosty, particularly if you don't look the part, or dare to handle the merchandise. But, of course, they all like a sale, and if you look like a potential buyer they will be very willing to help, even arranging to have your shopping taken back to your hotel.

If you want a new wardrobe, consider booking a personal shopper (through such hotels as the Principe di Savoia, Baglioni and Chateau Monfort). With discounts and outlet shopping, this service can pay for itself, and you get objective advice on which designers best suit your body shape. The busiest shopping times, particularly in and around the Quadrilatero d'Oro, are the fashion weeks at the end of February and the beginning of October.

jeans and sunglasses. North-east from the Giardini Pubb-lici, **Corso Buenos Aires** is the longest shopping street in Italy, packed with clothes, shoe shops, chain stores and discount outlets.

FACTORY OUTLETS

Most of the big factory outlets, which offer 20–75 percent off recommended retail prices, are inconveniently located in

Swimwear for the style-conscious male in the Quadrilatero d'Oro

the suburbs, but **Serraravalle** (www.mcarthurglen.it) is worth the trek. This is the biggest, most convenient out-of-town outlet (an hour away on a free shuttle bus from Foro Bonaparte, beside Piazza Castello (metro Cairoli). Closer to the centre, outlets pop up like mushrooms. The **Salvagente** outlet (Via Bronzetti 16; www.salvagentemilano.it) stocks heavily discounted fash-ion from Prada, Armani and other big names. On Piazza San Babilla (corner of Via Bagutta) is the **Kilo Fascion** (www.lilla internationalgroup.it) which, amusingly, sells the main designer brands by the kilo (the price depends on the weight).

INTERIOR DESIGN

Milan is also the world's leading centre for furniture and household design, and the city is home to a large number of stylish stores and showrooms. Some of the leading names sit along **Via Durini**, familiarly known as 'Design Street', and **Corso Matteotti**, both of which are south of the Quadrilatero d'Oro. Recommended brands include **Alessi** (for homeware and gadgetry; Via Manzoni 14; www.alessi.com), **Kartell** (for lamps, accessories and furniture; Via C Porta 1; www.kartell.com), and

Gourmet food shop

Cassina (for creative furniture and shelving; Via Durini 16; www.cassina.com). Design fans can also seek inspiration at the **Triennale Design Museum** (see page 50) and visit the city during the **Milan Furniture Fair**.

DEPARTMENT STORES

Milan's most central and upmarket department store and food hall is **La Rinascente** (www.rinascente.it) on Piazza del Duomo (daily until 10pm), beside the Duomo. La Rinascente offers stylish clothes, cosmetics and household goods as well as lingering views from the rooftop bars and food hall. Make the store your first shopping stop, if only to see what's on trend. **Coin** (http://en.coin.it), on Piazza Cinque Giornate, southeast of the centre, is a cheaper chain store for clothes and accessories, and is home to Eataly, a tempting Slow Food deli.

BOOKS AND MULTIMEDIA

Milan has a wide range of megastores, which are open seven days a week. The vast **Mondadori Multicenter** (www.mondadori store.it), occupying the Palazzo dei Portici in Piazza del Duomo, is a haven for book and gadget lovers. **Feltrinelli** (www.lafel trinelli.it) responds with big branches on Piazza del Duomo (on the corner with Via U. Foscolo) and the Stazione Centrale, both of which sell English-language books.

GASTRONOMY

Gourmets will enjoy the city's food shops, stacked with everything from home-cured hams, speciality risotto rice, herbs and honey to local wines, grappa and liqueurs. The legendary Milanese deli **Gastronomia Peck** (Via Spadari 9, near the Pinacoteca Ambrosiana; www.peck.it), is a showcase for the finest hams and cheeses, pasta, pastries, smoked wild salmon and spectacular truffles – all under the same roof, with a branded café nearby. **Ottimo Massimo** is a (smaller, more affordable; www.ottimomassimogourmet.it) rival, as are the impressive food halls at **Eat's Store** and **La Rinascente**, not to mention the **Van Bol & Feste** (www.vanbolandfeste.it) deli and café.

For delicious cakes and pastries, including a legendary *panettone*, the Milanese Christmas cake, go to **Pasticceria Marchesi** (www.pasticceriamarchesi.it), on Via Santa Maria alla Porta 13, an old-fashioned *pasticceria*. **Cova** (http://cova.com.hk) and **Biffi** (http://biffigalleria.it) are other chic, old-school alternatives, while the new boys include the **California Bakery** (www.californiabakery.it). The newer bakeries appeal to the Milanese love of novelty, brunch, bagels, bread and all-day eating. The bakeries also foster the illusion that local people could be hard-bitten New Yorkers in another incarnation. Wine connoisseurs will enjoy a visit to the **Enoteca Cotti** (www.enotecacotti.it) at Via Solferino 42, a long-established shop stocking around 1,000 fine wines and hundreds of grappas and liqueurs.

MARKETS AND ANTIQUES

Colourful street markets sell flowers, fruit, fashion and household goods. For clothing and accessories, including designer-label bargains, try the sprawling **Mercato di Viale**

Foodie listings

More information on the cafés and restaurants mentioned here can be found on page 108.

Fiera di Senigallia flea market

Papiniano at Porta Genova, held on Tuesday morning and all day Saturday. The Saturday **Fiera di Senigallia** (www.fieradisinigaglia.it) on **Ripa di Porta Ticinese** sells new and vintage clothing, CDs and accessories. The city **flea market** (metro Porta Genova) takes place on Sunday mornings. Every third Sunday of the month, except in August, the Brera hosts the **Mercato dell'Antiquariato** (Antiques Market), which also encompasses bric-a-brac and jewellery. But the biggest antiques market comes to the **Navigli** quarter on the last Sunday of the month (except July), with more than 400 stalls lining the banks of the Naviglio Grande canal.

ENTERTAINMENT

Milan is home to one of the world's most prestigious opera houses, along with scores of concert venues, art galleries and vibrant nightlife in Italy, matched by stylish bars and nightclubs.

Most information about events and entertainment has moved online and, reflecting this shift, Milan tourist board has revamped its website (www.turismo.milano.it). This should be your first port of call for finding out about forthcoming events. Look under the 'Happenings' section (in English). *Where Milan* magazine (free from the best hotels) is another invaluable source, and has an online edition (www.wheremilan.com). If you read Italian, Wednesday's edition of the *Corriere della Sera* newspaper has listings in the *ViviMilano* supplement, and *La Repubblica* does likewise in its Thursday *TuttoMilano* section.

OPERA

For many visitors Milan means opera. The Teatro alla Scala, or **La Scala** (www.teatroallascala.org; tel: 02 88791) as it is more familiarly known, hosts ballet and classical concerts as well as opera. The opera season runs from 7 December to July. Ballet and classical concerts are held here during the autumn months.

For information on ticket availability visit the website or call the Scala Infotel service on 02 7200 3744 (daily 9am–6pm). Seating plans and the season's programme can be viewed online. Tickets can be purchased either via the automatic telephone booking service (tel: 02 860 775; 24-hour service in four languages) up to two weeks before the performance, or online via the Teatro alla Scala website (credit card payments only, with 20 percent surcharge).

The central box office (daily noon–6pm) is in the Duomo metro station opposite the ATM public transport office. One month before performances take place all unsold tickets are put on sale here. Two hours before the performance, 140 numbered tickets for gallery seats are sold at the Evening Box Office, which is near the opera house. Any last-minute non-gallery tickets that are still available in the hour before the performance are sold with around a 25 percent discount.

CONCERTS

Milan is a deeply musical city, offering everything from classical concerts and choral music performances to live jazz and rock. Summer concerts in outdoor settings are increasingly popular. The best source of information for all music is the official Milan website (www.turismo.milano.it).

The **Conservatorio di Musica Giuseppe Verdi** at Via Conservatorio 12 (www.consmilano.it) hosts regular classical concerts in a former monastery from mid-September to June. The 1,400-seat **Auditorium di Milano** (www.laverdi.org) in the Ticinese quarter is home to the Symphonic Orchestra of Giuseppe Verdi and hosts symphony concerts, choral and chamber music, and jazz and light music.

Classical concerts are also held in churches throughout the city, notably in San Marco, San Simpliciano, Santa Maria del Carmine and San Maurizio. Summer open-air concerts take place at the Castello Sforzesco, in the gardens of the Villa Reale (www.amicidellamusicamilano.it), and in the courtyard of the Palazzo Marino (tel: 02 8846 2320). Pop and rock concerts are staged at San Siro stadium. Tickets for concerts and major events can be bought at stores such as Ricordi in the Galleria Vittorio Emanuele II.

La Scala's sumptuous interior

NIGHTLIFE

Milan's competing nightlife districts offer their own distinctive charms. Given the intriguing choice, it makes sense to focus on one area at a time. As a general rule, the centre offers classic Milanese nightlife while the Brera is both bohemian and sophisticated. The top hotel bars are classy rather than stuffy while the Quadrilatero is design conscious, the Navigli funky, and Corso Como flashy. The best time to spot film stars, footballers and fashion models is in the early evening, over cocktails at hip bars and cafés.

The **historic centre,** particularly the area around the cathedral, is always crowded

Happy hour

Cocktails are part of Milanese life, and Happy Hour often lasts from 6.30–9.30pm. The price of a drink may seem steep, but canapés and sometimes a whole buffet may be included and can provide a light supper in itself.

but offers classic Milanese haunts you would be foolish to shun. Begin a traditional bar crawl in **Camparino** (www.camparino.it), at the entrance to Galleria Vittorio Emanuele. This historic cocktail bar serves the best Campari in town, along with the juiciest olives. From here, resist the people-watching **Gucci Café** in the Galleria for a glorious sunset toast to Milan: the rooftop bars on the top of **La Rinascente** department store are irresistible. From here, saunter through the Galleria to La Scala to catch sight of the operatic crowd, probably sipping cocktails or Franciacorta sparkling wines, at the chic but contemporary **Cafe Trussardi**.

The neighbouring **Brera district** (metro Moscova or a pleasant walk down Via Verdi from La Scala) is both a slice of 'old Milan' and the most appealing place for cocktails. Apart from the vibrant **Via Fiori Chiari**, the preserve of fortune-tellers, illegal bag-sellers and cocktail bars, the nightlife options are less frenzied than in the Navigli canal quarter and more moodily Milanese than in the centre. **Cinc** (Via Formentini 5; www.cincbrera.it) overlooks one of the prettiest squares in the Brera, and is a lovely place for cocktails. Both friendly and quietly sophisticated, the bar serves classic concoctions made with the finest ingredients. The funky **Marc Jacobs** lounge bar (Piazza del Carmine) is better suited for the fashion and design crowd. When on Via Fiori Chiari, few can resist an organic ice cream at **Gelateria Amorino** (www.amorino.com).

Curiously, the **Quadrilatero fashion district** (metro San Babila or Montenapoleone) can be dead in the evening, apart from several exciting exceptions, particularly during Fashion Week. The *modellari*, the louche model-spotters (adorned with 'creative' glasses) often stalk their prey at the **Dolce & Gabbana Martini Bar** on Corso Venezia, and the rooftop views from the bar in the **Armani Hotel** are worth sampling if you feel sleek enough to face the 'fashion police'. **Armani Privé** (Via Pisoni 1) is the designer's branded nightclub, but expect a strict door policy. Far less fashion-obsessed is the frescoed bar at the **Four Seasons Hotel** or the cool bar at the **Bulgari Hotel**. **Conti Café** (Via Montenapoleone 19, tel: 02 7639 4934), tucked away down a courtyard, is a cosy (yet posey) lounge bar for a typical Milanese mix of backchat, cakes, sushi and Mediterranean-style pasta, preferably all at once.

The late-night hub of choice is the **Navigli canal quarter** (metro Porta Genova), which has a funkier, clubbier feel, especially in summer, and where you can dine late. While **Alzaia Naviglio Grande**, the main canal, is better for restaurants and a more sophisticated set, **Alzaia Naviglio Pavese** attracts a wilder crowd to the barge-bars moored on the banks.

More upmarket is the compact **Corso Como area** (metro Garibaldi), a buzzing nightlife area favoured by the fashion set and footballers on a roll. The hub is **10 Corso Como Café** (Corso Como 10, tel: 02 2901 3581; www.10corso como.com) a perennially fashionable lounge bar, restaurant, art gallery and concept store, perfect for a civilised late-night drink with the fashion and design crowd. If all this sounds too exhausting, simply while away an evening at the sophisticated **Principe Bar** (Hotel Principe di Savoia, metro Repubblica) or flaunt your style at the flashy **Just Cavalli Café** (Torre Branca, Parco Sempione; http://milano.cavalliclub.com).

SPORT

Football is a Milanese passion, and after Italy's positive team performance in Euro 2016, where they cruelly

San Siro Stadium

knocked out by Germany in a penalty shootout in the quarter finals, it is more popular than ever. The city has two major teams: Inter and AC Milan, both of which play at the Giuseppe Meazza San Siro Stadium, west of the city centre at Via Piccolomini 5 (metro Lotto, then tram 16). The teams play on alternate Sundays from September to May; for tickets visit www.acmilan.com and www.inter.it. (For details of the museum and stadium tour, see page 96.) The **AC Milan Megastore** in the Galleria Vittorio Emanuele is a good source of souvenirs and advice.

Another great spectator venue is the Formula One circuit at Monza, which hosts the **Italian Grand Prix** in September. Monza can be reached in 15 minutes by train from Stazione Centrale or Garibaldi.

For a break from the heat and traffic, head east to 'Milan's

On top of the Duomo

Sea'. Built in 1928 as a landing for seaplanes, it is a huge artificial lake with a water park, rowing regattas, canoeing and boating. The park is the place for jogging trails and opportunities for free climbing and mountain biking.

There are several golf courses, the best being **Milano Golf Club** (www.golfclub milano.it).

CHILDREN'S MILAN

Milan holds little fascination for young visitors, and unless they are immaculately behaved (and dressed) they won't be given a warm welcome in the fashion salons. Located in a historic Baroque building, Museo de Bambini (MUBA; www.muba.it) features exhibitions and workshops as well as cultural, artistic and leisure activities for children of all ages.

As for sightseeing, youngsters might enjoy clambering on the **roof of the Duomo**, going to the top of the **Torre Branca** or visiting the **Science Museum** (www.museoscienza.org), which exhibits huge boats, steam trains and aircraft.

Football enthusiasts will enjoy a match at Milan's **San Siro Stadium** or a visit to the **stadium museum** (Gate 21, Via Piccolomini 5; www.sansirotour.com; Apr–Oct daily 10.30am–5pm, variable times on match days). The museum has life-size statues of AC Milan and Inter heroes, and includes a visit to the stadium. When Milan palls, consider a day trip out on Lake Como, or short summer boat trips leaving from Milan's Navigli canal quarter. If all else fails, then Milanese cakes and ice cream should help alleviate the boredom.

CALENDAR OF EVENTS

Vibrant Milan offers everything from blockbuster art exhibitions in the Palazzo Reale to great music festivals. For more information on what's on, see www.turismo.milano.it.

6 January (Epiphany) *Corteo dei Magi* sees a historical procession of the Three Kings from the Duomo to Sant'Eustorgio.

February Carnival celebrating Sant'Ambrogio, continuing until the first Saturday of Lent. Parades with floats around the Duomo, religious services and children's events. **Mid-February** *Milano Moda Donna* Italian fashion designers present their autumn and winter collections in Milan; trade only, but coincides with concerts and fashion shows.

April *Salone Internazionale del Mobile* is the largest furniture exhibition in Europe. MiArt is one of the biggest European art shows.

May *Giro d'Italia* is a national cycle race held on a Sunday in late May. *Pittori sul Naviglio* is a two-day exhibition, when over 200 artists exhibit works along the banks of the Naviglio Grande. Milano Jazz Festival is a five-day music feast (www.ahumjazzfestival.com)

First Sunday of June Milan's *Festa dei Navigli* – antiques and craft stalls, boat races, street performers and concerts in the Navigli canal quarter. *Festival Latino-Americando* – three months of Latin American concerts and shows all over Milan (www.latinoamericando.it).

July and August *Milano Artemusica* is a six-week Festival of Ancient Music (www.milanoartemusica.com)held in churches such as San Simpliciano and Sant'Eustorgio.

September Italian Grand Prix – Formula One racing at Monza. *Milano Moda Donna* – spring and summer fashion collections (www.milano modadonna.it) at FieraMilano; trade only. *MITO Settembre Musica* is a month-long celebration of classical music.

November *The Maratona*, the Milan Marathon, is a 42-kilometre (26.2mile) trail through the city.

7 December Grand opening of Milan's La Scala opera season. This is also the *Festa di Sant'Ambrogio*, celebrating the city's patron saint. During the *Fiera degli O Bej O Bej*, held on **7 and 8 December**, market stalls are set up in the streets around the Basilica di Sant'Ambrogio.

EATING OUT

Milan's culinary scene caters for all tastes, from hearty Lombard stews to Michelin-starred creative cuisine, from sushi to fusion. The influx of immigrant workers from elsewhere in Italy in the 1950s introduced Milan to a range of regional cuisines, particularly Tuscan and southern Italian, such as Tuscan soups, Sicilian pastries and Neapolitan pizzas. A second wave of immigrants in the 1980s and 1990s, this time from further afield, has given Milan the widest range of ethnic eateries in Italy. Today you can find Japanese, Chinese, Thai, Indian, Middle Eastern, North African and American, amongst others.

LUNCH MILANESE-STYLE

The work ethic of Milan precludes the stereotypical Italian three-hour lunch break, although you can still linger in many places. However, in tune with the times, one popular trend is the rise of Slow Food quality at Fast Food rhythms, especially in the city centre. What's more, Milan shows there's no need to sacrifice style or quality to speed, even when restricted to lunch on the run.

Beside La Scala opera house, **Café Trussardi**, tucked into the Trussardi superstore, is a chic spot for a light lunch. Set in a former cinema, the food hall at **Eat's Store Excelsior** is another stylish place for a light lunch, as is the top floor of **La Rinascente** department store, which offers everything from a sushi bar to a mozzarella bar, overlooking the Duomo. Close by, **Ottimo Massimo** is a cross between a delicatessen and a café and serves superb Slow Food snacks all day long. In the Navigli canal quarter, **Luca and Andrea Café Bar** offers lovely salads at low prices, overlooking the Alzaia Grande waterfront. And just outside the Castello Sforzesco, **Van Bol & Feste** will set you up with a delicious foodie picnic to eat in the castle grounds.

Alfresco dining in the lively Brera neighbourhood

Though sushi may be the rage, classic Milanese fare manages to survive. It is highly varied, sourcing ingredients from nearby lakes, mountains and plains, and, unlike most Italians, local people prefer their food rich and creamy. Rice, rather than pasta, is the mainstay of their diet, grown on the vast paddy fields of the Po Valley. Lombardy also produces large amounts of corn, which is made into polenta (cornmeal) and served with many Milanese main courses in winter.

Meat and dairy produce are abundant, and butter, rather than olive oil, is used in Lombard cuisine. Risotto here is simmered in butter with onion, then cooked slowly with stock added bit by bit. Local cheeses, ranging from the parmesan-like Grana Padana to the creamy cow's-milk cheeses, appear on every menu, either enriching pastas and risottos or served on a platter with fresh bread and olive oil. Fresh herbs and vegetables, such as *porcini* mushrooms, artichokes, red chicory and asparagus, are key ingredients, grown in abundance and used

Buon appetito!

with fish, meat, risotto and pasta. Milan has the biggest fish market in Italy, ensuring a wide variety of freshwater fish and seafood.

WHERE TO EAT

Although traditionally a **ristorante** is smarter, more professional and expensive than a **trattoria**, the difference between the two can be negligible. An **osteria**, traditionally a tavern or inn serving wine and pasta, can nowadays range from traditional to hip, even if it often remains rustic and relaxed.

The ubiquitous **pizzeria** often extends to pasta and meat dishes but always serves 'proper' pizza bubbling hot from a wood-fired brick oven. The Milanese, like most Italians, prefer to eat pizza in the evening, and to accompany it with beer rather than wine. *Pizza a taglio*, sold by the slice with a variety of toppings, is the most popular Italian takeaway.

An **enoteca** or wine bar boasts a serious selection of fine wines, mostly available by the glass, and often served with a platter of cheese or charcuterie. A **tavola calda** is a basic self-service establishment with hot dishes (such as pasta and meat) while a **rosticceria** specialises in roast meats.

For a quick bite, go to a bar or café, where you can find a selection of rolls with savoury fillings and *tramezzini* (crustless, generously filled sandwiches).

WHAT TO EAT

As in the rest of Italy, restaurants (as opposed to *pizzerie*) offer four courses: *antipasti* (hors d'oeuvres), the *primo* (first course, usually pasta, risotto or soup), the *secondo* (main course of fish or meat), and the *dolce* (dessert), followed perhaps by cheese, coffee and a *digestivo*. Traditionally, you were expected to have at least three courses; nowadays, it's often acceptable to opt, for example, for a main course followed by a dessert.

ANTIPASTI

The selection of hors d'oeuvres will typically include an *antipasto di carne* or *affettati misti*, a selection of cold meats such as thinly sliced *prosciutto crudo* (Parma ham), *salame di cinghiale* (wild-boar salami), seasoned sausages and *bresaola* (air-dried beef), served with lemon, olive oil and black pepper. *Insalata di mare* (seafood salad) will be a plate of seafood such as prawns, mussels, squid and octopus; *antipasto di pesce* (fish) may be a selection of marinated seafood or lake fish such as *tinca* (tench) or *lavarello* (a white fish). Vegetable *antipasti*

DINING DOS AND DON'TS

Make reservations for popular restaurants, especially during major trade fairs. Opening times for lunch *(pranzo)* are 12.30pm to 2.30/3pm, and for dinner *(cena)* 7.30pm to 10/11pm, with some pizzerias and ethnic eateries open until midnight. For the best value, head for the Ticinese and Navigli quarters in the south of the city. Lunch is generally lighter and frequently cheaper than dinner. Be prepared for a nominal charge for bread and cover *(pane e coperto)*, plus an (often discretionary) service charge of around 10 percent. If service is not included, only round up the bill by a few euros unless the service has been spectacular.

Local rice dish risotto alla Milanese

are likely to feature *peperoni* (peppers), *zucchini* (courgettes), *melanzane* (aubergine or eggplant) and *carciofi* (artichokes).

PRIMI

Rice is prepared in dozens of different ways, enriched with fish, seafood, meat or vegetables. The ingredients vary according to the season. The most famous local rice dish is *risotto alla milanese*, made with Arborio or Carnaroli rice, slowly cooked with onions, beef marrow and stock, served with liberal amounts of butter and Parmesan cheese and – what makes it distinctly Milanese – flavoured and coloured with saffron. Other popular combinations are *risotto ai funghi*, cooked with mushrooms (particularly delicious are the *porcini* or wild mushrooms in the autumn) and *risotto alla pescatora* with prawns, squid, mussels and clams.

Pasta comes in all shapes and sizes, is often home-made and, like risotto, is served with a remarkable range of sauces. Along with the local specialities you can always find the long-standing favourites such as *al pomodoro*, tomato sauce flavoured with onion, garlic or basil, *alla carbonara*, with eggs, bacon, parmesan and pecorino cheeses, *al ragù*, the Neapolitan meat sauce, or *alle vongole*, with clams.

Soups can be a meal in themselves, especially the delicious *zuppa di pesce*, more of a fish stew than a soup and made with several types of fish. *Minestrone alla milanese*, a vegetable soup with rice and bacon, is widely available; other soups include *zuppa pavese*, a clear broth with egg and bread, and *zuppa di cipolle*, onion soup.

SECONDI

The classic Milanese meat dish is *osso bucco*, veal shank from milk-fed calves, slowly braised with wine, topped with *gremolada* (also spelt *gremolata*) – a paste of chopped garlic, lemon zest and parsley – and served with *risotto alla milanese*. Other local dishes include *cotoletta alla Milanese*, veal cutlet dipped in egg, coated in breadcrumbs and lightly fried in butter (which across the border in Austria goes by the name of *Wiener schnitzel*) and *cassoeula*, a wintry dish of pork cuts, sausage and savoy cabbage, cooked for several hours and usually served with polenta.

Beef, veal, ox tongue and spiced pork sausage are typical ingredients of *bollito misto* or boiled meats, often served with *mostarda di Cremona*, a sauce of mustard-flavoured preserved fruits. This meat dish is an acquired taste, as is the local *fritto misto*, a fry-up of veal liver, brains, lungs, sweetbreads and meat croquettes, usually served with

Osso bucco with polenta cakes

Tiramisù with sponge finger biscuits

mushrooms, artichokes or courgettes. You may also come across jugged hare, risotto with frogs' legs, and boiled snails prepared with fennel, anchovies and white wine.

For more conventional tastes, there is no problem finding simply cooked steak, pork, veal, lamb and poultry (especially duck, turkey and goose). The choice will vary according to the season. Any meat (or fish) *'alla milanese'* is likely to be coated in breadcrumbs and fried.

Milan may be landlocked, but a huge variety of fresh fish is delivered daily. As well as specialist seafood restaurants, many places offer just as much fish as meat. Freshwater fish is sourced from the River Po or Alpine lakes, and seafood from Italian shores and beyond. Commonly found on menus are *branzino* (bass), *orata* (bream), *sogliola* (sole), *gamberoni* (giant prawns), *calamari* (squid) and *vongole* (clams). Salted and dried cod *(baccalà)* is used in dozens of recipes. Many restaurants use frozen fish, and the more upfront ones will indicate this with a star against the item. Smaller fish are served whole at a fixed price, but the larger species will be charged by the *etto* (100g/3.5oz), and it's wise to check the price before ordering.

Main courses often come with *contorni* (vegetables); salads are ordered and served separately and are invariably *verde* (green) or *mista* (mixed). Vegetarian restaurants have been

springing up, but most restaurants offer meat-free
rice dishes at the very least. You could try grilled vegetab
an *antipasto*, followed by a risotto or pasta with fresh asparag
or *porcini* (ceps); alternatively you might wish to splash out on
the 13-course tasting menu at Joia (see page 112), one of the
best vegetarian restaurants in Italy.

DOLCI

Depending on the restaurant, for a dessert (*dolce*) you may be
offered anything from a fruit salad or *gelato* (ice cream) to a
choice from a trolley of elaborate home-made desserts and
cakes. Panettone, the domed cake containing eggs, butter, rai-
sins and candied fruit, was originally a Milanese dessert, but
is now a famous Christmas cake found throughout the country. Many restaurants serve tiramisù (literally 'pick-me-up'),
the alcoholic chocolate and coffee gateau from the Veneto.
As an alternative, you could do as many Milanese do and buy
an ice cream from a superb *gelateria* such as Amorino (on Via
Fiori Chiari 9, in the heart of the Brera), or Grom on Via Santa
Margherita 16, near La Scala.

Cheese platters are laden with delicious Lombard varieties,
from creamy Mascarpone, blue-veined Gorgonzola, and soft and
pungent Taleggio, to fresh, creamy Stracchino, tangy Provolone
Valpadano and the hard Grana cheese produced in the Po Valley.

WINES AND LIQUEURS

Outside Italy, Lombardy is not considered one of the celebrated
wine-producing regions, and, in terms of fame, its prestige
can't match that of neighbouring Piedmont. However, the rise of
Franciacorta, a delightful area on the shores of Lake Iseo, near
Brescia, means that Italians are fully aware of the excellence of
Lombardy's wines. Although hilly Franciacorta also produces
Bordeaux-style reds, it is best known for its Champagne-style

A leisurely family meal in the Navigli quarter

wines, considered Italy's finest sparkling varieties.

Franciacorta DOCG makes an excellent aperitif, with recommended producers including Ca' del Bosco, Il Mosnel and Bellavista. Lombardy also produces dry, smooth reds from Valtellina, grown on steep terraces on the Italian/Swiss border. The region's most productive zone is Oltrepò Pavese, in the Po Valley south of Pavia, noted for some good Pinots and robust Barbera; the region also produces fruity white Riesling and Moscato dessert wine.

Restaurants invariably offer wines from other regions, such as Barolo from Piedmont or Brunello from Tuscany, while gourmet inns will also list a smaller selection of international wines. House wine, *vino della casa*, is usually acceptable and always reasonably priced. In cheaper places it's served in litre or half-litre carafes or jugs.

A good meal is frequently concluded with a *digestivo*, such as a brandy, grappa (powerful fruit or herb-flavoured firewater) or *limoncello*, a lemon liqueur.

TO HELP YOU ORDER...

A table for one/two/three please **Un tavolo per una persona/per due/per tre**

I would like... **Vorrei...**

The bill please **Il conto per favore**

What would you recommend? **Cosa ci consiglia?**

...AND READ THE MENU

aglio garlic	**maiale** pork
agnello lamb	**manzo** beef
aragosta lobster	**melanzane** aubergine
basilica basil	**olio** oil
birra beer	**olive** olives
bistecca steak	**pane** bread
burro butter	**panna** cream
calamari squid	**patate** potatoes
carciofi artichokes	**peperoni** peppers
cinghiale wild boar	**pesce** fish
cipolle onions	**piselli** peas
coniglio rabbit	**pollo** chicken
cozze mussels	**polpo/pólipo** octopus
fagioli beans	**pomodori** tomatoes
fagiolini green beans	**prosciutto** ham
finocchio fennel	**riso** rice
formaggio cheese	**salsiccie** sausages
frittata omelette	**spinaci** spinach
frutti di mare seafood	**tonno** tuna
funghi mushrooms	**uova** eggs
gamberetti shrimps	**verdure** vegetables
gamberi prawns	**vino** wine
gelato ice cream	**vitello** veal
insalata salad	**vongole** clams
lumache snails	**zucchini** courgettes

PLACES TO EAT

The prices indicated are for a three-course evening meal per person, including cover charge and service but excluding wine.

€€€€ over 80 euros   €€€ 50–80 euros
€€ 30–50 euros   € below 30 euros

HISTORIC CENTRE

Antico Ristorante Boeucc €€€ *Piazza Belgioioso 2, tel: 02 7602 0224,* www.boeucc.it. The oldest restaurant in Milan, Boeucc has served guests of the calibre of Verdi, Donizetti and Toscanini. Nowadays, it is renowned for impeccable service and classic Milanese cuisine, such as saffron-flavoured *risotto alla Milanese.* Closed for lunch on Saturday and Sunday.

Café Trussardi, €€–€ *Piazza della Scala 5, tel: 02 8068 8295,* www.trussardi.com. Set beside La Scala, and tucked into the ground floor of the designer superstore, this café is a sleek, people-watching spot for a coffee, snack, light lunch or cocktails and nibbles. On the floor above is the brand's exorbitant but exceptional two-Michelin-starred gastrodome **Trussardi Alla Scala** (tel: 02 8068 8201).

Cracco €€€€ *Via Victor Hugo 4, tel: 02 876 774,* www.ristorante cracco.it. Arguably the best restaurant in Milan, Carlo Cracco's two-Michelin-starred restaurant offers outstanding creative cuisine. The *menu degustazione* might offer Asian-style dishes or more traditional asparagus ravioli with black truffles.

Eat's Store Excelsior €–€€ *Galleria del Corso 4, tel: 02 7601 5176.* This former cinema is now an upmarket store for niche luxury brands, including chocolate. The ground floor is home to a popular café and food hall, which offers wine tastings, light meals and a tempting array of Italian deli treats.

Al Mercante €€€ *Piazza Mercanti 17, tel: 02 805 2198,* www.rist orantealmercante.it. Set in a remodelled Gothic mansion on the only medieval square in Milan, this is a charming spot, with tables spilling onto the square. Tuck into classic Northern Italian cuisine, Milanese meat dishes and fresh fish. Sunday lunch only.

La Milanese €€–€€€ *Via Santa Marta 11, tel: 02 8645 1991.* Genuine Milanese fare is served in this traditional trattoria, where you can always find *osso buco* (braised veal shanks), *risotto alla milanese*, *cotoletta alla milanese* (breaded and fried veal) and fine Lombard wines. Closed Sun.

Ottimo Massimo € *Via Victor Hugo, tel: 02 4945 7661,* www.ottimo massimogourmet.it. This cafe-meets-delicatessen is a rival to the famous Gastronomia Peck (Via Spadari 9) around the corner. Whereas Peck focuses on deli cheeses, meats, pastries and wine, Massimo encourages you to try them in the café (and it's less pricey here). What's more, the all-day opening means you can have brunch, lunch or afternoon tea here, too.

Peck Italian Bar €€ *Via Cesare Cantù 3, tel: 02 869 3017,* www.peck. it. A bar/bistro open from lunch to 8pm for light meals, cheeses, charcuterie, pastries and cocktails. At lunch time it's popular with traders from the nearby Stock Exchange. Prices reflect the fact that the produce and wines are from Peck, Milan's top food emporium. Closed Sunday.

La Rinascente €–€€ *Piazza Duomo, tel: 02 885 2471,* www.rina scente.it. The top (seventh) floor of Milan's smartest department store is a wonderful food emporium offering everything from a juice bar and salad bar, to a sushi bar, Champagne bar, and an Obikà mozzarella bar (see page 111). Several cafés and restaurants have outside terraces overlooking the Duomo's spires.

Sant'Ambroeus €–€€ *Corso Matteotti 7, tel: 02 7600 0540,* www. santambroeusmilano.it. This long-established café is convenient for La Scala and is an attractive place for cocktails and grazing on oysters, salmon or Parma ham. Open all day until 1am.

CASTELLO SFORZESCO AND NORTHWEST

ATMosfera €€ *tel: 02 4860 7607,* www.atm.it, book at https://atm osfera.atm.it. Dine in a plush, old-fashioned tram which takes you around the city and down to the Navigli quarter. There are three set menus of four courses – meat, fish or vegetarian – each costing €65 including wine. Reservations generally need to be made 2–3 months beforehand, unless you book the whole tram. The departure point is Piazza Castello.

Just Cavalli Hollywood €€–€€€ *Via Camoens at the Torre Branca, tel: 02 311 187,* http://milano.cavalliclub.com/en. This glitzy supper-club/nightclub is owned by Roberto Cavalli and cast in his flashy image. The restaurant side gets mixed reviews for its (often indifferent) food and service, but on a good night fans and fashionistas are simply content to soak up the glamorous atmosphere. Open from 7pm until around 5am, this place really comes alive during Fashion Week.

Triennale Design Café €–€€ *Via Alemagna 6, tel: 02 913 6683,* www.triennale.org. Set in the Design Museum overlooking Parco Sempione, this is an engaging if minimalist place. Chef Michelangelo serves a creative, seasonal, all-day menu, producing anything from truffled pasta to saffron risotto, as well as simpler dishes. The show kitchen enables you to watch the chefs in action. Closed on Mondays.

Van Bol & Feste € *Foro Bonaparte 71, tel: 02 8909 3182,* www.vanbol andfeste.it. Set just outside the Castello Sforzesco, which leads to Parco Sempione, this Neapolitan deli, café and bistro serves delicious pastries, breads, savouries, salads, wine and gastro treats, including plum cake and ices. Drop in if planning a picnic in the castle grounds or park. Open daily until 11pm.

THE BRERA

Latteria San Marco €–€€ *Via San Marco 24, tel: 02 659 7653.* This former *latteria*, or dairy, is small, homely and unpretentious. Expect simple Lombard fare, including pasta, meatballs and greens from the owner's vegetable patch. The *trattoria* is frequented by journalists from the nearby *Corriere della Sera* newspaper. Closed at weekends.

Nabucco €€€ *Via Fiori Chiari 10, tel: 02 860 663,* www.nabucco.it. Enjoy elegant cuisine in the atmospheric heart of the Brera. Dine by candlelight, or alfresco on summer evenings. Try Nabucco's *antipasti*, the sautéed *zucchini* (courgette) flowers filled with fresh ricotta and pesto, *linguine all'astrice* (pasta with lobster), or the fresh fish. The restaurant is open until 11.30pm.

Obikà €€ *28 Via Mercato 28 (corner of Via dei Fiori Chiari), tel: 02 8645 0568,* www.obika.com. The rapidly expanding Obikà chain is dedicated to authentic Campanian Bufala mozzarella, ranging from sweet and creamy to strong and smoked. All are displayed within a minimalist, sushi bar-inspired interior and served with salami, smoked wild salmon, or Sicilian grilled vegetables.

La Torre di Pisa €€ *Via Fiora Chiari 21, tel: 02 804 483,* www.trattoria torredipisa.it. Overlooking a bustling Brera street, this homely trattoria has been serving authentic Tuscan fare since 1959. The rustic setting remains, full of paintings and bottles of wine. Try the home-made Tuscan pastas, the Florentine steaks and the ice cream with pine kernels from Pisa.

NORTHEAST, EAST AND STAZIONE CENTRALE

Acanto €€€€ *Hotel Principe di Savoia, Piazza della Repubblica 17, tel: 39 026 2301,* www.dorchestercollection.com. One of the best restaurants in Milan, this is supremely confident northern Italian cuisine created by Fabrizio Cadei. Expect superb service, a stylish, people-watching heaven, and a great brunch too. The restaurant is popular with George Clooney, the Beckhams and Monica Belucci.

Armani Nobu €€€€ *Via Pisoni 1, tel: 02 7231 8645,* www.nobu restaurants.com. This is a chic sushi haunt in the heart of 'Armani-hood', home to Giorgio's superstore and part of the chain of Japanese master chef Nobu Matsuhisa. Fashionistas flock here for the sushi fusion – with Japanese and South American influences.

Bice €€€ *Via Borgospesso 12, tel: 02 795 528*, www.bicemilano.it. Set in the heart of the exclusive shopping quarter, this is a favourite, unfaddish spot for fashionable Milanese. The elegant cuisine features Tuscan, Lombard and traditional Northern Italian dishes. Try the risotto with cheese and pears or saffron and ceps. Closed on Sunday evenings.

Brek € *Piazzetta Ugo Giordano, tel: 02 7602 3379*. This restaurant tucked away behind Piazza San Babila is one of the few cheap options in the Quadrilatero fashion district. The reliable self-service chain is the place for simple pasta, pizza and risotto, salads and fresh fruit. Pleasant setting and you won't face any cover or service charges. Closed Sunday.

La Caffetteria € *Villa Nechi Campiglio, Via Mozart, tel: 02 763 40121*. Set in a pavilion in the charming grounds of Villa Necchi, this café is more than a pit stop. The changing menu is short but good, with pasta, risotto and plates of charcuterie and salad, as well as cakes and good coffee. The Modernist villa-museum isn't bad either. Open daily 10am–6pm.

Corso Como 10 €€ *Corso Como 10, tel: 02 2901 3581*, www.10corso como.com. The focus is an elegant courtyard restaurant that serves a great Sunday brunch, as well an eclectic mix of sushi and international dishes. The chic lounge bar, art gallery and concept store is perfect for afternoon tea or a late-night drink.

Da Giannino-L'Angolo d'Abruzzo €–€€ *Via Pilo 20, tel: 02 2940 6526*. This charmingly old-fashioned, family-run trattoria showcases specialities from Abruzzo. Expect a warm welcome and hearty portions.

H Club Diana €€ *Hotel Sheraton Diana Majestic, Viale Piave, tel: 02 2058 2034*, www.sheratondianamajestic.com. Near metro stop Porta Venezia, this is one of the city's most popular spots for a huge Sunday brunch (12.30–3pm) but happy hour is also a lure.

Joia €€€ *Via Panfilo Castaldi 18, tel: 02 2952 2124*, www.joia.it. Expect vegetarian and seafood haute cuisine in an elegant setting just north of the Giardini Pubblici (Public Gardens). Run by a guru of vegetarian food, Joia serves such dishes as ravioli with peppers, buckwheat gnocchi and carob bean ice cream. Book in advance. Closed on Sundays.

Ombre Rosse € *Via Plinio 29, tel: 02 2952 4734*, www.enotecaombre rosse.com. An old-fashioned wine bar dating back to the 1930s, when lorries came with tanks full of Chianti. Today, it offers more than 400 wines (including by the glass) accompanied by Tuscan and Parma hams, smoked pork and salami, *pasta e fagioli* (pasta and beans), cassoulet or vegetable couscous. Closed on Sundays.

Ristorante Rubacuori €€€ *Chateau Monfort, Corso Concordia 1, tel: 02 7767 6708, www.ristoranterubacuori.it, metro San Babila (and walk).* The name means 'heart-stealer' and it does, with a series of playful dining rooms matched by the creativity of Pasquale d'Ambrosio, an inventive Neapolitan chef. Cooking is healthy but not fussy, with southern influences and the freshest fish or mozzarella. Stay overnight (see page 138) for the best breakfast in Milan.

SOUTH: NAVIGLI, TICINESE, ZONA TORTONA

El Brellin €€ *Vicolo del Lavendai, Alzaia Naviglio Grande, tel: 02-5810 1351;* www.brellin.com. This romantic canalside corner of old Milan (including a former wash-house) offers a traditional menu celebrating Milanese cuisine.

Circle € *Via Stendhal 36, tel: 02 4229 3745,* www.circlemilano.com. Combining restaurant, lounge bar and brunch spot by the Diesel headquarters, Circle lies in the newly hip Zona Tortona design district. The Saturday brunch (until 4pm) attracts a trendy crowd, as do the buzzing late nights from Tuesday to Friday. Closed on Monday evenings.

Al Coniglio Bianco €€ *Alzaia Naviglio Grande 12, tel: 02 5810 0910,* www.alconigliobianco.it. A charmingly rustic canalside inn (with a pretty terrace) with regional food to match, ranging from saffron risotto to pumpkin flan, artisanal pasta, polenta, cutlets, *osso buco* and fish dishes. Closed Tuesday.

L'Officina 12 €€ *Alzaia Naviglio Grande 12, tel: 02 8942 2261*, www.officina12.it. Rustic yet resolutely urban, this funky canalside restaurant has a private garden, a stylish bar (happy hour 7-9.30pm), pizzeria and reliable range of dishes from cheese flans to stuffed pasta and steaks. Closed Monday lunch.

Luca & Andrea Café Bar € *Alzaia Naviglio Grande 34, tel: 02 5810 1142*. Come here for a light lunch of salads while sitting canalside, or to graze at happy hour.

Osteria Delbinari €€€ *Via Tortona 1, tel: 02 8940 9428*. A delightful inn, with an equally charming garden, in the new Zona Tortona design district, near metro stop Porta Genova. Milanese dishes such as saffron risotto and *cotoletta alla Milanese* vie with vegetarian dishes. Open daily.

Premiata Pizzeria € *Alzaia Naviglio Grande 2, tel: 02 8940 0648*, http://mypizzeriaristorante.com. Expect a reliable pizzeria (with a wood-fired oven) at the Darsena end of the canal, with garden and terrace. Other options are cured meats, cheeses, pastas, steaks or salads.

Sadler €€€-€€€€ *Via Ascario Sforza 77, tel: 02 5810 4451*, www.sadler.it. Set in the Navigli canal district, Carlo Sadler's two-Michelin-starred temple to gastronomy offers inspired creative cuisine, including Oriental influences. Open evenings only and closed August. For exceptionally good value try its stylish offshoot, **Chic' n Quick** (tel: 02 8950 3222; same address).

MILANESE CAFÉS AND ICE CREAM

These include places for snacks, brunch, pastries, ices and tea.

Caffe Cova €-€€ *Via Montenapoleone 8, tel: 02 7600 5599*, www.pasticceriacova.it. A Milanese institution, this elegant pastry shop (*pasticceria*) sits in the heart of the Quadrilatero fashion district. The tearooms are beyond fashion, with their tiny pastries (*pasticcini*) popular with size zero supermodels and the ladies who lunch. Stop for a coffee and chocolate cake or sample the *panettone*.

California Bakery € *Piazza Sant'Eustorgio 4, tel: 02 3981 1538,* www.californiabakery.it. A small, family-run chain with a creative Italian take on such American staples as bagels, brunch and cheesecake. Tuck into bagels with mozzarella or Parma ham, try the weekend brunch, or choose their picnic hamper.

Gelateria Amorino € *Via Fiori Chiari 9, Brera,* tel:02 9153 2598, www.amorino.com. Near metro stop Moscova, this is arguably the best ice-cream parlour in Milan, with pure, organic yet creative flavours.

Pasticceria Biffi €–€€ *Corso Magenta 87, tel: 02 4800 6702,* www. biffipasticceria.it. An old-fashioned pastry shop that rivals Caffe Cova in its sweet heritage (*marrons glaces*, pralines and Christmas *panettone*) but also serves a savoury *aperitivo* buffet.

That's Bakery € *Via Vigevano 41, tel. 02 839 4890,* www.thatsbakery. com. Reflects the craze for cupcakes and Americana. Enjoy lunch-time sandwiches, high tea or brunch with an Italian take on English country-chic.

A–Z TRAVEL TIPS

A Summary of Practical Information

A

ACCOMMODATION (see also Hotels on page 135)

Milan has an increasing number of design hotels, boutique bolt-holes and even quirky B&Bs, along with business hotels. During trade fairs, prices rocket. If there is any flexibility regarding your Milan trip, check the schedule of international fairs on the Milan tourism website (www.turismo.milano.it). Some of the best deals are available online, including in August, when many Milanese head for the coast, or the weekends, when business hotels are virtually empty.

When making a reservation, a deposit of one night's stay, payable by credit card, is usually requested. Failure to inform the hotel in advance of cancellation will normally incur the loss of the deposit. Room rates include local taxes and service charges.

I'd like a single/ double room/twin beds **Vorrei una camera singola/matrimoniale/due letti singoli**
with bath/shower **con bagno/doccia**
What's the rate per night? **Quanto costa per notte?**

AIRPORTS

Milan has three main airports. Easily the most convenient for the centre is **Linate** (tel: 02 232 323; www.milanolinate-airport.com), 10km (6 miles) east of Milan, which handles mainly domestic and European flights. The Starfly shuttle (www.starfly.net) operates a half-hourly service to Milan's Stazione Centrale, taking 25 minutes, and the cheaper No. 73 bus (www.atm.it) departs every 10 minutes (between 5.35am and 12.35am) to Piazza San Babila in the city centre. The X73 express bus covers the same route but with stops only at Dateo. You can also take the Air Bus, a shuttle service that links Milan's central railway station with the airport. See www.atm.it for more details.

Malpensa airport (tel: 02 232 323; www.milanomalpensa-airport.com), 50km (31 miles) northwest of the city, services national, international and intercontinental flights. The airport is linked to Milan's Cadorna station by the Malpensa Express train (www.malpensaexpress.it). Trains run every half-hour and take 40 minutes. The Malpensa Shuttle (www.malpensashuttle.it) and the Malpensa Bus Express (www.autostradale.it) run regular coach services to Stazione Centrale, taking 50–60 minutes.

Orio al Serio airport (tel: 035 326 323; www.orioaeroporto.it) is at Bergamo, 48km (30 miles) northeast of Milan, and is used by Ryanair and other low-cost airlines. A half-hourly shuttle bus service runs to Stazione Centrale, taking an hour, and is operated by Autostradale (tel: 035 322 915; www.autostradale.it) and Orio Shuttle (www.orioshuttle.com).

Could you please take these bags to the bus/train/taxi?
Puo portarmi queste valige fino all'autobus/al treno/al taxi per favore?
What time does the train/bus/tram leave for the city centre?
A che ora parte il treno/Pullman/tram per il centro?

B

BICYCLE HIRE

The BikeMi public service (www.bikemi.com) enables cyclists to pick up a bike from one of over 300 stations, cycle for up to two hours and leave it at any other BikeMi station. But cycling is more stressful than pleasurable, so opt for an organised bike ride with Ciclolobby (tel: 02 6931 1624, www.ciclolobby.it).

BUDGETING FOR YOUR TRIP

Milan is one of the most expensive cities in Italy, but flights could be as low as €100. Expect to pay €140 upwards for a decent double room, €60–120 for a double in a simple hotel or B&B. Typically a good three-course meal without wine costs from €30–50 upwards; a sandwich with a drink and coffee €8–12; a coffee €1.50–3; a cocktail with nibbles or buffet included €8–15. Drinks at the bar are often cheaper than those served at a table. A metro or tram ticket is €1.50.

The Open Wi-Fi Milano (http://info.openwifimilano.it) offers free Wi-Fi connection in many piazzas and streets. There is also a free indoor Wi-Fi network in many public buildings such as libraries, museums and the city hall.Entry fees to museums, attractions and gardens vary from €2–15.

Money-saving tips include buying a transport and museum pass, exploring churches, and grazing on canapés and buffets over cocktails. Bakeries and food halls make enjoyable (and affordable) lunch stops. In summer the city stages a number of free outdoor concerts.

C

CAR HIRE (See also Driving)
The best rates are usually found online. The major rental companies have outlets at Milan's airports and at the Stazione Centrale. A small car will cost from around €200 a week, including third-party liability and taxes, but excluding insurance excess. Drivers must present their own national driving licence or one that is internationally recognised.

CLIMATE
The best time to go to Milan is spring, early summer or autumn. July and August are uncomfortably hot, with temperatures of around 30ºC (86ºF), and in August many businesses, restaurants and shops close down. Winter months tend to be foggy and cold,

and snow is not uncommon. The chart below shows the maximum average temperatures in Milan.

	J	F	M	A	M	J	J	A	S	O	N	D
°C	5	8	13	18	23	27	29	29	24	17	10	6
°F	40	46	56	65	74	80	84	85	75	63	51	43

CRIME AND SAFETY

Take precautions against pickpockets. Leave important documents and valuables in the hotel safe, and keep a firm hold of handbags, especially around the Central Station. For insurance purposes, theft and loss must be reported immediately to the police.

I want to report a theft. **Vorrei denunciare un furto.**
My wallet/passport/ticket has been stolen. **Mi hanno rubato il portafoglio/il passaporto/il biglietto.**

D

DISABLED TRAVELLERS

For information on accessibility, including suggested itineraries, visit www.milanopertutti.it (tel: 02 330 2021). Milan's public transport company, ATM, has information for disabled travellers on its website (www.atm.it). Access-Able Travel Source (www.access-able.com) is a database of travel agents from around the world with experience in accessible travel.

DRIVING

Milan is served by an extensive motorway network connecting the city with the rest of the country, but driving within the city, with its chaotic traffic, congestion charge, and one-way streets, is best avoided.

Congestion Charge. To discourage cars from entering the city centre, the **Area C** (Congestion Charge Area) covers the centre and operates from Monday to Friday, 7.30am to 7.30pm, when a daily €5 fee is charged to enter the 'Cerchia dei Bastioni', defined as being the area 'within the bastions', the ring of 16th-century Spanish walls which, confusingly, barely exist as they were mostly demolished long ago. (For more on Area C, see www.comune.milano.it.)

Parking. Finding a parking space in Milan is notoriously difficult. The centre is subject to a ZTL *(zona a traffico limitato)* scheme, meaning that traffic and parking are tightly regulated. For information visit www.atm.it (some of the details are in Italian only).

Rules of the road. Drive on the right, overtake on the left. Unless otherwise indicated, speed limits are 50kmh (30mph) in towns and built-up areas, 90110kmh (5568mph) on main roads and 130kmh (80mph) on motorways *(autostrade)*. Headlights must be kept on during the day on motorways and state roads *(strade statali)*. Seat belts are compulsory in the front and back, and children should be properly restrained. The use of hand-held mobile phones while driving is prohibited. The blood alcohol limit is 0.08 percent, and police occasionally make random breath tests.

Breakdowns. In case of accident or breakdown call 113 (General

---

I've had a breakdown **Ho avuto un guasto**
There's been an accident **C'è stato un incidente**
Fill it up please **Faccia il pieno per favour**
super/normal **super/normale**
unleaded/diesel **senza piombo/gasolio**
Where's the nearest car park? **Dov'è il parcheggio
    più vicino?**
Can I park here? **Posso parcheggiare qui?**
Are we on the right road for...? **Siamo sulla strada
    giusta per...?**

Emergencies) or the Automobile Club of Italy. The club has an efficient 24-hour service and an English-speaking service (tel: 803 116). **Petrol.** Some service stations close for lunch and on Saturday afternoons and Sundays, but there are plenty of 24-hour stations with self-service pumps; cash and major credit cards are accepted.

E

ELECTRICITY

220V/50Hz AC is standard. Sockets take two-pin, round-pronged plugs. American 110V appliances need a transformer.

EMBASSIES AND CONSULATES

Australia: Australian Consulate General, Via Borgogna 2, tel: 02 7767 4200, www.italy.embassy.gov.au.

Canada: Canadian Consulate General, Piazza Cavour 3, Milan, tel: 02 6269 4238, www.canadainternational.gc.ca; emergency call collect (613) 996 8885.

New Zealand: New Zealand Consulate General, Via Terraggio 17, tel: 02 721 70001, www.nzte.govt.nz.

UK and Ireland: British Consulate General, Via San Paolo 7, tel: 02 723 001, www.britain.it.

US: US Consulate General, Via Principe Amedeo 2/10, tel: 02 290 351, http://milan.usconsulate.gov.

EMERGENCIES

Police 113
Carabinieri 112
Fire 115
Ambulance 118
General Emergency 113

Local doctors are on call for emergencies from Monday to Friday, on Saturday from 2–8pm and on Sunday from 8pm–8am, tel: 02 34567.

GAY AND LESBIAN TRAVELLERS

Milan is young, cosmopolitan and, for Italy, free-thinking so argu-ably offers the best gay scene in Italy. What's more, given Milanese open-mindedness, a number of clubs blur the line and are both gay- and straight-friendly.

Useful resources are www.gayfriendlyitaly.com and www.guida gay.it. More official is Arcigay Milano (Via Bezzecca 3; tel: 02 5412 2225; www.arcigaymilano.org, Italian only), the main point of contact.

GETTING THERE

By air. British Airways (www.ba.com) operates frequent flights from Heathrow to both Linate and Malpensa airports and to Mal-pensa from Birmingham and Manchester. Services from Stansted and Bristol to Orio al Serio airport at Bergamo are run by Ryanair (www.ryanair.com). EasyJet (www.easyjet.com) flies from Gatwick to Linate and Malpensa, and Flybe (www.flybe.com) from Birming-ham and Manchester to Malpensa, with Air One connecting Gat-wick and Malpensa. Alitalia (www.alitalia.com) flies from Heathrow and London City to Linate.

From the US there are direct flights from main cities, including New York, Boston and Los Angeles.

By car. The quickest route to Milan from the UK channel ports (1,040km/650 miles) takes a minimum of 12 hours. For route plan-ning visit www.viamichelin.com, which gives details of the cost of petrol, road tolls and the Swiss motorway tax. To bring your car into Italy, you need a valid international or national driving licence, car registration documents, red warning triangle in case of breakdown, safety vest and a national identity sticker.

By rail. The quickest route from the UK is by Eurostar (tel: 08432 186 186, www.eurostar.com) to the Gare du Nord in Paris, changing to the Gare du Lyon for trains to Milan. For information in the UK on tickets, rail passes and booking, contact International Rail (tel: 44 (0)871 231 0790, www.internationalrail.com).

GUIDES AND TOURS

Citysightseeing Milano offers hop-on hop-off open-topped bus tours (including a commentary in English, tel: 02 867 131, www. milano.city-sightseeing.it). Three-hour coach sightseeing tours, bookable online, depart from Piazza del Duomo (www.autostradale. com). Zani Viaggi offers a 'Footsteps of Leonardo' tour, as well as tours to Lake Como and Lake Maggiore (tel: 02 867 131, www.zani viaggi.it).

For canal tours, contact Navigli Lombardi (tel: 02 667 9131, www.naviglilombardi.it). A tour with Adartem guarantees access to Leonardo's *Last Supper* or to the battlements of the Castello Sforzesco (tel: 02 659 7728, www.adartem.it). Book a tour of the cathedral spires through the Duomo or Milan tourist office.

H

HEALTH AND MEDICAL CARE

All EU countries have reciprocal arrangements for reclaiming the costs of medical services. UK residents should obtain the EHIC (European Health Insurance Card), available from post offices or online at www.ehic.org.uk. This does not cover emergency repatriation costs or additional expenses. To cover all eventualities a travel insurance policy is advisable, and for non-EU residents essential. For insurance claims keep all receipts for medical treatment and any medicines prescribed.

Vaccinations are not needed, but take sunscreen and mosquito repellent in summer. The water is safe to drink but most visitors and locals drink mineral water.

If you need a doctor (*medico*), ask at a pharmacy or your hotel. For serious cases or emergencies, dial 118 for an ambulance or head for the *Pronto Soccorso* (Accident and Emergency) of the local hospital, which will also deal with emergency dental treatment.

Pharmacies. A pharmacy *(farmacia)* is identified by a green cross. Locations of pharmacies open after-hours are posted on all pharmacy doors or tel: 800 801 185. An all-night service is available at the Stazione Centrale (Central Station) on the first-floor gallery (tel: 02 669 0935). Italian pharmacists are well trained to deal with minor ailments and, although they do not stock quantities of foreign medicines, they can usually supply the local equivalent.

I need a doctor/dentist **Ho bisogno di un medico/dentista**
Where is the nearest chemist? **Dov'è la farmacia più vicina?**

L

LANGUAGE
Staff in the main hotels and shops normally speak English. In the more out of the way places a smattering of Italian will come in useful, and any attempt will be appreciated.

M

MEDIA
Newspapers. The main English and foreign newspapers are available on the day of publication from major news-stands and the Feltrinelli and Mondadori media megastores (see page 88). For city listings consult the excellent Milan City Tourism website www.turismo.milano.it and the complementary site www.comune. milano.it.

Television and radio. Most Milan hotels provide satellite TV, broadcasting 24-hour English-speaking news channels. The Italian state TV network, RAI (Radio Televisione Italiana) broadcasts three channels, RAI 1, 2 and 3, and a huge number of private channels pour out soaps, films and quiz shows. The state-run radio stations (RAI 1, 2 and 3) mainly broadcast news, chat and music.

MONEY

Currency. The unit of currency is the euro (€), divided into 100 cents. Euro notes come in denominations of 500, 200, 100, 50, 20, 10 and 5; coins come in denominations of 2 and 1, then 50, 20, 10, 5, 2 and 1 cents.

Exchange facilities. Banks offer the best rates, followed by exchange offices and hotels. Some exchange offices *(cambi)* offer commission-free facilities, but check that the exchange rate is not exorbitant. They are usually open Mon–Sat 8.30am–7.30pm.

Credit cards and cash machines. The major international credit cards are accepted in the majority of hotels, restaurants and stores. ATM cash machines *(Bancomats)* are widespread and have instructions in English. Since ATMs and credit cards have become the norm, travellers' cheques are no longer widely accepted.

> I want to change some pounds/dollars **Desidero cambiare delle sterline/dei dollari**
> Do you accept travellers' cheques? **Accetta travellers' cheques?**
> Can I pay with a credit card? **Posso pagare con la carta di credito?**

O

OPENING TIMES

Banks generally open Mon–Fri 8.30am–1.30pm and 2.30–4pm, but hours vary; a few open continuously from 8am–4pm.

Museums' and art galleries' hours vary but closing day is normally Monday.

Churches usually close from noon to 3pm or later, though the Duomo is open all day.

Shops are generally open Mon–Sat from 9am–1pm and 3.30–7.30pm, but many close on Monday mornings. The large stores are open all day from 9.30 or 10am–7.30 or 8pm, and sometimes on Sundays too. Food stores often close on Monday. Many shops close in August.

P

POLICE

The city police or *Polizia Urbana* regulate traffic and enforce laws, while the *Carabinieri* are the armed military police who handle law and order. In an emergency the *Carabinieri* can be reached on 112 – or you can ring the general emergency number, 113. In the case of stolen goods, contact the *Questura* (police station) at Via Fatebenefratelli 11, tel: 02 62 261, metro MM3 Turati.

Where's the nearest police station? **Dov'è il posto di polizia più vicino?**

POST OFFICE

The central post office, offering money transfer and banking facilities, is at Via Cordusio 4, and is open Mon–Fri 8.20am–7.05pm, Sat

Where's the nearest post office? **Dov'è l'ufficio postale più vicino?**

I'd like a stamp for this letter/postcard **Desidero un francobollo per questa lettera/cartolina**

8.20am–12.35pm. The Stazione Centrale (tel: 02 6707 2150) has a post office open Mon–Sat 8.25am–7.10pm. Stamps *(francobolli)* can also be purchased from tobacconists (marked with a T sign). First-class mail *(posta prioritaria)* guarantees delivery within 24 hours within Italy and three days for EU countries. For other information, visit www.poste.it.

PUBLIC HOLIDAYS

Banks, offices, museums, galleries and most shops close on the days listed below. When a national holiday falls on a Thursday or a Tuesday, Italians may make a *ponte* (bridge) or long weekend.

1 January New Year's Day
6 January Epiphany
March/April Easter Monday
25 April Liberation Day
1 May Labour Day
2 June Republic Day
15 August *Ferragosto*, Feast of the Assumption
1 November All Saints' Day
7 December Feast of Sant'Ambrogio (patron saint)
8 December Immaculate Conception
25 December Christmas Day
26 December Santo Stefano, St Stephen's Day

R

RELIGION

Like the rest of Italy, Milan is primarily Roman Catholic. There are congregations of all the main religions. The Duomo has several services a day; for information visit www.duomomilano.it. Access is not allowed if you are dressed in sleeveless shirts, short shorts or other skimpy attire.

S

SMOKING

Smoking is not allowed in indoor public places. This includes bars and restaurants, and is widely respected.

T

TELEPHONES

Given Italians' dependence on mobile phones (the highest ownership in Europe) telephone boxes are in short supply. Even many bars and small businesses often operate solely by mobile phone. When phoning abroad, dial the international code, followed by the city or area code and then the number. The off-peak rate for international calls applies Mon–Sat 10pm–8am, Sun 1pm–Mon 8am. For an English-speaking operator and international reverse-charge calls dial 170, and for international directory enquiries dial 176. Numbers beginning with 800 are free. Italian area codes have all been incorporated into the numbers, so even if calling within Milan you must include the code. Note that Italian telephone numbers do not have a standard number of digits – it can be anything from four to ten.

Mobile phones. In order to function within Italy, some mobile phones need to be activated with a roaming facility or 'unblocked' for use abroad. Check with your mobile company, including confirming fees and networks to see which local network is best, then set the phone to the cheapest network on arrival. If in Italy for some time, consider purchasing an Italian SIM 'pay as you go' phone (scheda pre-pagata) with a new mobile number. The SIM card can be bought from any mobile shop in Italy; you will need your passport or ID card. To keep your mobile number, sign up with www.uk2abroad. com who will divert calls to your Italian SIM card.

Country codes. Australia +61; Ireland +353; Italy +39; New Zealand +64; UK +44; US and Canada +1.

TIME ZONES

Italy is one hour ahead of Greenwich Mean Time (GMT). From the last Sunday in March to the last Sunday in October, clocks are put forward one hour.

The chart below shows times across the globe when it is midday in Milan.

New York	London	**Milan**	Jo'burg	Sydney
6am	11am	**noon**	1pm	8pm

TIPPING

In restaurants a *coperto* or cover charge ranging from €1.50–5 is usually charged for service and bread. Tipping is not taken for granted, though a bit extra will always be appreciated. For quick service in bars, leave a coin or two with your till receipt when ordering. In restaurants service is usually included in the bill. Taxi drivers do not expect a tip, but appreciate a few euros. At hotels you could tip porters €1 for each bag.

Thank you, this is for you **Grazie, questo è per lei**
Keep the change **Tenga il resto**

TOILETS

Main train and bus stations have public toilets, usually with attendants who charge a small fee. Otherwise, it is generally a case of using the facilities of a café or bar. *Signori* is Men, *Signore* is Women.

Where are the toilets, please? **Dove sono i gabinetti, per favore?**

TOURIST INFORMATION
Italian Tourist Offices Abroad
Australia: Level 2, 140 William Street, East Sydney NSW 2011, www. enit.it

Canada: 69 Yonge Street, Suite 1404, Toronto (Ontario) M5E 1K3, tel: 416 925 4882, http://toronto.enit.it

UK: 1 Princes Street, London W1B 2AY, tel: 020 7408 1254, http:// london.enit.it

US: New York: 686 Park Avenue, New York, NY 10065, tel: 212-245 5618; http://newyork.enit.it.

Chicago: 3800 Division Street. Stone Park, IL 60165, tel: 312-644 0996; http://chicago.enit.it.

Los Angeles: 10850 Wilshire Blvd., Suite 575, Los Angeles, CA 90024, tel: 310-820 1898; http://losangeles.enit.it.

Milan Tourist Offices
Milan's best tourist office is the InfoMilano (Galleria Vittorio Emanuele II, corner piazza della Scala; tel: 02 8845 5555; Mon–Fri 9am–7pm,until 6pm on Sat and 10am–6pm on Sun). City listings, including events, can also be viewed on the reliable official city websites www.turismo.milano.it and www.comune.milano.it .

The Stazione Centrale (Central Station) has an affiliated IAT tourist office (tel: 02 7740 4318; Mon–Fri 9am–6pm, Sat 9am–1.30pm and 2–6pm, Sun and hols 9am–1.30pm, 2–5pm, located by platform 13/14). Milan's airports at Linate, Malpensa and Orio al Serio all have tourist information offices.

TRANSPORT
Milan has an efficient public transport network, run by ATM (Azienda Trasporti Milanesi; tel: 800 808 181, toll-free in Italy, daily 7.30am–7.30pm, www.atm.it).

Metro, buses and trams. The metro is the fastest and most practical means of getting around. Metro stations are marked by a large red 'M'. The Metropolitana Milanese (MM) has four underground lines plus the Passante Ferroviario (PF), which serves suburban areas. The lines are distinguished by different colours: M1 is red, M2 green, M3 yellow, M5 lilac and PF is blue.

Trains run every few minutes from 6am until 12.30am. Free transport maps are available from Milan airports, railway stations, and the tourist information offices. Tickets are available from machines at stations, and from newsagents, and are also valid for tram and bus routes. A single ticket costs €1.50 and is valid for 90 minutes for one metro journey plus unlimited tram and bus routes. Savings can be made by buying a book of 10 tickets. Tourist tickets, valid for 24 or 48 hours (€4.50 and €8.25 respectively) or €11.30 for a week, can be used on the ATM bus, tram and metro network. Tickets must be validated every time you board a train or bus. Failure to do so may incur a fine.

Trains. Milan's main railway station is the Stazione Centrale (Central Station), a major rail junction, which is almost fully renovated, with new ticket offices, a media megastore and shopping mall. For train information, see the official Italian rail website at www.trenitalia.com, where tickets can be booked online. Or book through Italian specialists in the UK, such as International Rail (tel: 44 (0)871 231 0790, www.internationalrail.com).

Italian trains are cheap compared to those in the UK and the US and the network has made great strides while maintaining reasonable fares. Local trains are slow but fast intercity trains deliver speed, comfort, service and reliability. They are well worth the supplements levied but require reservations. The high-speed **Frecciarossa** trains serve the line linking Milan with Turin, Bologna, Florence, Rome and Naples. Depending on the class, expect free Wi-Fi, reclining seats, complimentary magazines, Illy coffee and snacks. **Frecciabianca** trains serve the line linking Milan with Venice, Turin and Trieste, while **Frecciargento** operates on the Venice and Verona route.

Milan is now linked to Rome in only 3 hours, and to Florence in 2 hours 10 minutes. There are also regular fast services from Milan to towns on the lakes, such as Stresa and Como. It is sensible to buy your ticket early (or online, as above), as the Central Station ticket office invariably has long queues, even if there are dedicated lines for the fast services. Alternatively, use the automatic ticket-issuing machines. Return tickets offer no saving on two singles. Before boarding the train, frank the tickets at the yellow machines at the near end of the platform. Failure to do so may result in a fine.

Taxis. Taxis are white and can be found at ranks around the city. For a Radio Taxi tel: 02 7777 or 02 8585. There are extra charges on Sundays and holidays, at night and for luggage. Make sure the taxi has a meter and uses it, and beware of touts without meters near airports and train stations. If in doubt, ask for an estimated price before starting the journey. Some taxis now accept credit cards.

When's the next bus/train to...? **Quando parte il prossimo autobus/treno per...?**
single (one-way) **andata semplice**
return **andata e ritorno**
first/second class **prima/seconda classe**
What's the fare to...? **Qual'è la tariffa per...?**

V

VISAS AND ENTRY REQUIREMENTS

For citizens of EU countries a valid passport or identity card is all that is needed for stays of up to 90 days. Citizens of the US, Canada, Australia and New Zealand require a valid passport.

Visas *(permesso di soggiorno)*. For stays of more than 90 days a visa or residence permit is required. Contact the Italian embassy in your country.

Customs. Free exchange of non-duty-free goods for personal use is allowed between EU countries. Those from non-EU countries should refer to their home country's regulating organisation for a current list of import restrictions.

Currency restrictions. Tourists may bring an unlimited amount of Italian or foreign currency into the country. On departure you must declare any currency beyond the equivalent of €10,000, so it's wise to declare sums exceeding this amount when you arrive.

W

WEBSITES AND INTERNET ACCESS

Milan's official site is www.turismo.milano.it, with its companion site covering the province and the city, www.comune.milano.it.

Other informative English-language websites for visitors include: http://ciaomilano.it, which has reasonable advice and general listings; and www.wheremilan.com, which is especially good for shopping and dining listings (also in magazine form in the best hotels). For Milan's delightful, intimate 'house museums', such the Museo Bagatti Valsecchi, see www.casemuseomilano.it. A useful site with detailed info on the city's museums is www.milan-museumguide.com. The city's official website, www.comune.milano.it, provides practical information ranging from events to the congestion charge. If you're interested in Milanese football, see www.sansiro.net.

Internet access. Most hotels have Wi-Fi access, but not always free of charge. Free Wi–Fi networks are widely available across the city, even inside public buildings. Detailed information and map of hotspots can be found at www.turismo.milano.it.

There are also internet points at the airports, in the Stazione Centrale, at FNAC on Via Torino, and in the Mondadori Multicenter, a multimedia store on Piazza del Duomo, with long opening hours.

A city brimming with some of Italy's best luxury hotels now has designer-branded boltholes and stylish boutique hotels to match. The choice is far less inspired at the mid-range, family and budget end where small, appealing, inexpensive hotels are hard to find. A few stylish B&Bs are emerging, though rarely in the centre.

Given Milan's business reputation, hotel prices often drop at the weekend and in July and August, when the stifling weather sends the Milanese to the coast or lakes, but many hotels close in August. Many of the best rates and special offers are only available online. If there's a major fair on, hotels will be scarce. During the fashion, design and tourism shows (mid-January, mid-February, April, end of June and end of September) prices rocket, and you will need to book well in advance. If you arrive without a reservation, the IAT office (see page 131) can supply hotel information but will not make the booking for you. However, the tourist offices at the Stazione Centrale and at Linate and Malpensa airports do provide booking facilities.

The symbols indicate the rough cost of a twin room, on a B&B basis, in high season.

€€€€	over €350
€€€	€200–350
€€	€150–200
€	up to €150

HISTORIC CENTRE

Gran Duca di York €€ *Via Moneta 1, tel: 02 874 863*, www.ducadiyork. com This is one of Milan's most appealing three-star hotels, set in a 200-year-old *palazzo* within easy walking distance of the Duomo. Pleasant rooms with designer furnishings and minibars with complimentary soft drinks.

Park Hyatt €€€€ *Via Tommaso Grossi 1, tel: 02 8821 1234*, www.milan. park.hyatt.com. A stone's throw away from the Duomo, with windows overlooking the Galleria Vittorio Emanuele II, this elegant Hyatt has a dramatic foyer, soaring glass dome and a restaurant, La Cupola, offering all-day dining. For bold city views opt for a rooftop suite with a large terrace.

Spadari al Duomo €€€ *Via Spadari 11, tel: 02 7200 2371,* www.spadari hotel.com This was one of Milan's first designer hotels. Close to Piazza del Duomo, it remains stylish, with a pretty, pale-blue colour scheme, light walnut furnishings, an arty ambience and a welcoming atmosphere.

Star €–€€€ *Via dei Bossi 5, tel: 02 801 501,* www.hotelstar.it. Sink into a small, family-run hotel close to La Scala, the Duomo and the Castello. Some rooms have whirlpool baths or sauna showers. Breakfasts are generous, there is free Wi-Fi in public areas and the service is particularly helpful. You can get great last minute deals here.

Straf €€€–€€€€ *Via San Raffaele 3, tel: 02 805 081,* www.straf.it. An artful designer hotel with exposed concrete, burnished brass and high-tech functionality. There's a cool cocktail bar and live music on occasions. While standard rooms are not spacious, the 'wellbeing rooms' compensate with aromatherapy and spa facilities.

Town House Galleria €€€€ *Galleria Vittorio Emanuele II, tel: 02 8905 8297,* www.sevenstarsgalleria.it. Located above Prada, this luxury small hotel overlooks Milan's grandest gallery. Rooms come with a personal butler who is on constant call to unpack, order a Bentley or book tickets for La Scala.

CASTELLO SFORZESCO

Ariosto €–€€€ *Via Ariosto 22, tel: 02 481 7844,* www.hotelariosto. com. This Art Nouveau *palazzo* has a quiet, inner courtyard, which houses the most desirable rooms – some have their own sauna and whirlpool. Facilities include bar, cafeteria, conference room, garden, and free Wi-Fi access.

London €–€€ *Via Rovello 3, tel: 02 7202 0166,* www.hotellondonmilano. com. Pleasantly old-fashioned, family-run hotel, ideally placed on a quiet street between the Castello and the Duomo. Bedrooms are small and nothing special, offset by a cosy lounge, free Wi-fi and friendly, helpful staff.

Palazzo Segreti Hotel €€€ *Via San Tomaso 8, tel. 02 4952 9250,* www. palazzosegreti.com. This striking boutique hotel occupies a patrician palace between La Scala and the Castello Sforzesco (metro Cairoli). Has soft lighting, funky contemporary furnishing, parquet floors and splashes of colour, plus a wine bar serving fine wines, Lombard cheeses and charcuterie. There's also a day spa.

NORTHWEST AND BRERA

Antica Locanda Solferino €€€ *Via Castelfidardo 2, tel: 02 657 0129,* www.anticalocandasolferino.it. An intimate little hotel in the heart of the Brera with a faintly rustic feel. The distinctive rooms are furnished with Art Nouveau antiques, floral fabrics and original prints – along with flat-screen TVs and Wi-fi.

Bed and Bread € *Via Vetta d'Italia 14, tel: 02 468 267,* www.bedand bread.it. South of the emerging City Life district, this simple B&B has three double rooms and a communal room with TV, internet and library. Generous breakfasts feature home-made bread, jam and cakes. The Duomo is 2km (1 mile) away and can be reached by bus or tram.

NORTHEAST, EAST AND STAZIONE CENTRALE

Armani Hotel €€€€ *Via Manzoni, tel: 02 883 8888.* This hotel epitomises the anonymous luxury for which Armani is famous, and fashionistas are fans of the duplex suites and spa. With floor-to-ceiling windows, the bold rooftop bar is Armani at his sophisticated best.

Hotel Aspromonte € *Piazza Aspromonte 12–14, tel: 02 236 1119,* www. hotelaspromonte.it. This easy-going, good-value Art Nouveau hotel is furnished in a sober, modern style, and equipped with Wi-fi. In summer breakfast is served in the interior garden. Slightly off the beaten track (metro Loreto).

Baviera €–€€ *Via P. Castaldi 7, tel: 02 659 0551,* www.hotelbaviera. com. Expect a traditional hotel with friendly staff, renovated public areas and good-value guest rooms just north of the public gardens. Convenient for the station and local restaurants.

Bulgari €€€€ *Via Privata Fratelli Gabbia 7b, tel: 02 805 8051,* www. bulgarihotels.com. Bulgari, of jewellery fame, run this contemporary designer hotel. Overlooking the Botanical Gardens, and with its own garden, spa and lap pool, this chic retreat has stylish bedrooms decorated in tones of brown and beige. The garden-view, minimalist restaurant attracts an elegant crowd, as does the smart bar. Services include a personal shopper, luggage unpacking, and High Tea with Champagne.

Carlton Hotel Baglioni €€€–€€€€ *Via Senato 5, tel: 02 77 077,* www.baglionihotels.com. This discreet luxury hotel is perfect for the Quadrilatero, with an entrance leading to Via della Spiga, 'fashion central'. The Terrazza Baglioni restaurant is also a fashionista favourite. The public rooms, in sedate English-club style, are matched by classic bedrooms, a contemporary boutique (linked to up-and-coming designers), and a handy online Milan guide, accessed on an iPhone.

Casa Mia € *Viale Vittorio Veneto 30, tel: 02 657 5249.* This small, friendly budget hotel near Piazza Repubblica and the Giardini Pubblici (Public Gardens) is 15 minutes' walk from the Duomo. The street is busy, but most rooms overlook a quiet courtyard.

Chateau Monfort €€€–€€€€ *Corso Concordia 1, tel: 02 77 6761,* www.hotelchateaumonfort.com. Within walking distance of San Babila and the Fashion District, this quirky 'urban chateau' is a reaction against the bland homogeneity of the business hotels. Expect fairytale touches such as secret alcoves, fake hunting trophies, beds evoking an enchanted forest, and an atmospheric spa. Dine in Rubacuori (see page 113) for a meal to remember, or just enjoy the best breakfast in Milan.

Echo €€–€€€, *Viale Andrea Doria, tel: 02 67 891,* www.starhotels. com–hotels/echo. Facing the Central Station, this hotel combines style with eco-chic. Designed in soothing earth tones, the Echo is equally popular with the business and leisure crowds. The Central Station area has been revamped.

Grand Hotel et de Milan €€€€ *Via Alessandro Manzoni 29, tel: 02 723 141*, www.grandhoteletdemilan.it. A prestigious location a stone's throw from La Scala and sumptuous rooms add to the desirability of this heritage hotel. Founded in 1863, the hotel's illustrious guests include Giuseppe Verdi, Ernest Hemingway and Maria Callas.

Hotel Principe di Savoia €€€€ *Piazza della Repubblica 17, tel: 02 62 301*, www.hotelprincipedisavoia.com. The revamped bedrooms are contemporary, stylish and individualistic while the suites include one with a Pompeiian pool and another grand chandeliered affair that was David Beckham's Milan home. The staff may be the friendliest and most professional in the city. Movers and shakers flit between the rooftop pool and spa, before cocktails in the moody Principe Bar, and dinner in Acanto, the superb gastronomic restaurant.

San Francisco € *Viale Lombardia 55, tel: 02 236 0302*, www.hotel-san francisco.it. A three-star hotel east of the Stazione Centrale which is worth the out-of-the-way location for the reasonable prices. Simple, well-cared-for, air-conditioned rooms are complemented by a bar/breakfast room with a leafy garden at the back.

Starhotels Anderson €€–€€€ *Piazza Luigi di Savoia, tel: 02 669 0141*, www.starhotels.com. Literally steps from the railway station, the Anderson makes a convenient stopover. This contemporary, well-refurbished hotel has a fitness centre, elegant bedrooms, good food and courteous service.

Town House 31 €€€ *Via Carlo Goldoni 31, tel: 02 70 156*, www.town househotels.com. Set in a residential quarter, Town House 31 is a chic home-from-home for fashionistas, offering a combination of comfort, cutting-edge design and convivial atmosphere. An arty, ethnic ambience embraces Chinese temple arches, dark oriental furniture and cream decor enlivened by African touches. The breakfast room has a long communal table, and also serves as a popular *aperitivo* bar, with a tropical garden wine bar. A hot favourite during fashion weeks.

Una Hotel Tocq €€–€€€ *Via de Tocqueville 7D, tel: 02 62 071*. For night-owls, this is the perfect location for exploring the bars on Corso Como. Bedrooms are bland but comfortable. The contemporary bar is fun at *aperitivo* time while the restaurant works for both a business and leisure crowd.

WEST OF CENTRE

Antica Locanda dei Mercanti €€€ *Via San Tomaso 6, tel: 02 805 4080,* www.locanda.it. This romantic 18th-century bolthole is equidistant from the cathedral, castle and designer shops of the Quadrilatero. The gorgeous, discreet guest rooms are individually furnished with lovely classic fabrics and free Wi-fi. Optional breakfasts are taken in your room – or in the case of four of the rooms, on the private terrace.

Antica Locanda Leonardo €€–€€€ *Corso Magenta 78, tel: 02 4801 4197,* www.anticalocandaleonardo.com. A charming boutique hotel set back from the smart Corso Magenta, very close to Leonardo's *Last Supper*. It is run by a delightful Japanese and Italian couple. Reception is a pretty salon overlooking the courtyard. Peaceful bedrooms are a decent size for Milan and simply furnished, mainly with traditional fabrics, 1930s furniture and cherry wood floors.

King €€€ *Corso Magenta 19, tel: 02 874 432,* www.hotelkingmilano. com. Civilised and welcoming three-star on the elegant Corso Magenta. Rooms have traditional furnishings and floral fabrics. The energetic (or foolhardy) will appreciate the free use of the hotel's bikes.

Palazzo delle Stelline €€–€€€ *Corso Magenta 61, tel: 02 481 8431,* www.hotelpalazzostelline.it. A 15th-century monastery and former orphanage, this is now a congress centre/hotel with modern rooms set around a large cloister. The location is excellent, on the upmarket Corso Magenta. Dining options range from a café/bar with an attractive garden terrace to the gourmet Gli Orti di Leonardo restaurant. Rooms are good value given the location, but reception staff could be more welcoming.

Ariston €€–€€€ *Largo Carrobbio 2, tel: 02 7200 0556,* www.ariston hotel.com. 'The first ecological hotel', the Ariston provides air-purified, minimalist rooms, drinks made with purified water, organic breakfast products and free bikes for guests to explore the city. The rather dreary looking nine-storey block is set back off a busy street, about a 10-minute walk, or five-minute bike ride, from the Duomo.

Corte del Naviglio €€–€€€ *Via Lodovico il Moro 117, tel: 02 8918 1292.* On the Naviglio Grande, 5km (3 miles) southwest of the historic centre, the hotel is well served by public transport. Surrounded by a leafy garden, this former villa was the summer residence of the Marquess of Barona in the 17th century. Pretty, tiled guest rooms (with free Wi-fi) are decorated in different shades of yellow and blue. Offers live music including jazz.

Maison Borella €€–€€€ *Alzaia Naviglio Grande 8, tel: 02 5810 9114,* www.hotelmaisonborella.it. A charming canalside boutique hotel convenient for the Navigli nightlife and for the emerging Tortona fashion district. Reliable restaurant.

Uptown Palace €€€ *Via Santa Sofia 10, tel: 02 305 131,* www.preferred hotels.com. This sophisticated, upmarket hotel is close to the Basilica of San Lorenzo but is also handy for the Duomo and the shopping districts. Understated and family-friendly, it has a panoramic restaurant terrace (with creative cuisine) and a pampering spa.

INDEX

Berlitz POCKET GUIDE

MILAN

Fourth Edition 2017

Editor: Tom Fleming
Author: Susie Boulton
Head of Production: Rebeka Davies
Pictures: Paolo Burtoni
Cartography Update: Carte
Update Production: AM Services
Photography Credits: Alamy 67; Corbis 5MC, 6ML, 7TC, 57, 63, 95; Dreamstime 55, 77; Fotolia 4TC, 5MC, 6TL, 6MC, 7M, 7MC, 9R, 26, 35, 82, 92, 102, 103, 104; Glyn Genin/Apa Publications 4ML, 4TL, 5T, 5TC, 5M, 5M, 7T, 7M, 8R, 9, 11, 13, 19, 20, 24, 29, 30, 31, 32, 33, 34, 37, 38, 40, 41, 42, 43, 45, 46, 47, 48, 50, 52, 60, 66, 68, 69, 71, 73, 74, 76, 78, 87, 88, 90, 96, 99, 100, 106; iStock 81, 84; Jerry Dennis/Apa Publications 4MC, 6TL, 8L, 15, 16, 18, 53, 54, 59, 64, 65, 75; Sergio Piumatti 23
Cover Picture: AWL Images

Distribution
UK, Ireland and Europe: Apa Publications (UK) Ltd; sales@insightguides.com
United States and Canada: Ingram Publisher Services; ips@ingramcontent.com
Australia and New Zealand: Woodslane; info@woodslane.com.au
Southeast Asia: Apa Publications (SN) Pte; singaporeoffice@insightguides.com .
Hong Kong, Taiwan and China: Apa Publications (HK) Ltd; hongkongoffice@insightguides.com

Worldwide: Apa Publications (UK) Ltd; sales@insightguides.com

Special Sales, Content Licensing and CoPublishing
Insight Guides can be purchased in bulk quantities at discounted prices. We can create special editions, personalised jackets and corporate imprints tailored to your needs. sales@insightguides.com; www.insightguides.biz

All Rights Reserved
© 2017 Apa Digital (CH) AG and Apa Publications (UK) Ltd

Printed in China by CTPS

Contact us
Every effort has been made to provide accurate information in this publication, but changes are inevitable. The publisher cannot be responsible for any resulting loss, inconvenience or injury. We would appreciate it if readers would call our attention to any errors or outdated information. We also welcome your suggestions; please contact us at: berlitz@apaguide.co.uk
www.insightguides.com/berlitz

speaking your language

phrase book & dictionary
phrase book & CD

Available in: Arabic, Brazilian Portuguese*, Burmese*, Cantonese Chinese, Croatian, Czech*, Danish*, Dutch, English, Filipino, Finnish*, French, German, Greek, Hebrew*, Hindi*, Hungarian*, Indonesian, Italian, Japanese, Korean, Latin American Spanish, Malay, Mandarin Chinese, Mexican Spanish, Norwegian, Polish, Portuguese, Romanian*, Russian, Spanish, Swedish, Thai, Turkish, Vietnamese
*Book only

www.berlitzpublishing.com